# THE WAY FORWARD

# The Way Forward

*Implementing Trauma Responsive Care for Intellectual and Developmental Disability Professionals*

Kevin Aldridge, MA

LIBRARY OF CONGRESS CATALOGING-IN-PUBLICATION DATA
Names: Aldridge, Kevin D., author.
Title: The way forward : implementing trauma responsive care for
intellectual and developmental disability professionals / Kevin
Aldridge, MA.
Description: Kingston, N.Y. : NADD Press, [2023] | Includes bibliographical
references and index. |
Identifiers: LCCN 2022045776 (print) | LCCN 2022045777 (ebook) | ISBN
9798985336658 (paperback) | ISBN 9798985336665 (epub)
Subjects: LCSH: Social work with people with disabilities. | Social work
with people with mental disabilities. | Communication in services for
people with disabilities. | Psychic trauma. | Social service--Practice.
Classification: LCC HV1568 .A379 2023 (print) | LCC HV1568 (ebook) |
DDC
362.4/04--dc23/eng/20221123
LC record available at https://lccn.loc.gov/2022045776
LC ebook record available at https://lccn.loc.gov/2022045777

Copyright © 2023 by Kevin Aldridge

Published by NADD Press
321 Wall Street, Kingston, N.Y. 12401

ISBN 979-8-9853366-5-8 (paperback)
ISBN 979-8-9853366-6-5 (e-book)

Cover and book design by Mark Sullivan

# contents

This book is dedicated to my wife
*Debra R. Aldridge*
who sustained me for almost four decades
and whose memory sustains me still.

# foreword

Years ago, I had a client who worked in the physical sciences. One day as I was talking to him about balance — a word therapists just love to use — he mentioned offhandedly, "Well, of course there are two kinds of balance, you know."

"Really?! That's amazing, tell me more!" I calmly and professionally blurted. Surprised that his therapist was suddenly so interested in mechanical physics, he obliged me and explained that one type of balance is stationary. If you put your coffee mug on a table, the mug won't move unless something happens to the table or the mug. The mug doesn't have to exert any energy or change position to stay on the table, it just ... sits there. This is called static balance.

The other kind, he explained, is dynamic balance. When we ride a bike, we're usually not perfectly centered. We're constantly shifting our weight slightly as the wheels roll over the road. In fact, that's what makes bike riding hard at first; we feel this movement and overcorrect, lurching too far in one direction and then the other, eventually falling over. After doing that a few times, we decide we're not going to wobble so much this time, by God, and steer rigidly — right into a crash. But with time and practice, we learn the feel of continuous movement. We take in the feedback, and we lightly tilt accordingly, always adjusting and continuing to steer. In this way, we stay upright and move forward in equilibrium.

I've used this example for many years with just about every client I've ever had since that day. I think this is because, in the United States at least, we seem obsessed with the idea of achieving balance. And I think we see it in just those terms: an achievement. Once we've reached it — phew! Job done. And my clients often have this idea that when they find the perfect formula — X number of minutes spent each day for each task, exactly perfect eating and exercise and parenting and partnering and yoga and kale, and on and on — then, life will be in balance. All they'll have to do is maintain that equation every day, forever, like mugs on a table.

The truth, of course, is that we're all on bikes. And not the fancy featherweight Tour de France kind, either, but rusty old things, with flattish tires, gears that lock and chains that fall off. Every so often, we get thrown into a ditch (looking at you, 2020). So, the challenge on these rickety bikes is to keep moving forward, allowing for constant adjustment and change, within a range that allows that dynamic balance, that eventual equilibrium.

Feedback and change — that's what so much human activity is really about, and organizations are just groups of humans, after all. So dynamic balance is a pretty sound way to describe the endless, delicate movement of organizations, and *that* is what this book is all about — moving people, moving activities, moving objectives and outcomes, following a path that recognizes, accounts for, and supports trauma. Kevin writes about change. Change sounds great, on paper, but in truth we typically resist it. I think this is because change requires bravery — not in terms of our future, but in terms of our past. In order to seriously consider changing something about how we do what we do, we have to tolerate the idea that there's something that isn't working or at least doesn't work any longer. Maybe there is something we haven't done, or worse, something we did do that went wrong. I find that no human being really likes to do this, but I think it's especially difficult for people who work in human services. We try so hard, most of us, to get it right — because if we don't, other people suffer. And for leadership, it's even harder. The lives affected may not be only their consumers, but also their workers and their stakeholders. Dozens or even hundreds of people may bear the brunt of their missteps. How terrifying that must feel.

I think what strikes me most about *The Way Forward* are its reassurance and its humility. Kevin speaks about management from lifelong interest, deep knowledge, and wide professional experience in every sector — as an executive, a state official, a case manager, an international consultant, and, apparently, an unstoppable baseball nerd. He uses examples of things he learned from the successes and failures of others but also the successes and failures of his own. This humility allows for a lot of grace. I think that is what may make this book easy to pick up and, more importantly, easy to start implementing — it's safe. It's hopeful. "You can do this," it says. "You can keep moving forward."

The book is also full of research and scientific validation of its ideas. It's organized so you can read it through, starting with the theory and moving to the steps, or you can skip ahead to what interests you first and work backward if you want. There are things you can start trying right away — the "Monday morning list," as we refer to it. (There are also an unreasonable number of sports metaphors.) Kevin uses concepts and theories an MBA will recognize and appreciate in terms any team member, from managers to frontline staff, can understand and relate to. Speaking of managers, Kevin also includes a lot of "Supervision 101," basic yet under-taught skills and strategies for those universal management problems. In human service agencies, supervisors are often frontline staff who've been promoted with little to no training in the art and science of management. Kevin is a brilliant, intuitive leader who makes some of his wisdom plain and usable here. Most of all, it lays out the path ahead for the future of trauma-responsive human services. It helps to feel that however wobbly the ride has been, especially recently, we can regain that dynamic balance.

Close to my heart is the frequent discussion of the stresses and needs of the staff. At Aldridge Palay Consulting, we have long believed, and trained our agencies and customers, that the trauma suffered by consumers is often matched by the traumas your work-force has endured. Making an entire agency sensitive to this — helping one another to feel *safe, connected, and in control* — may offer healing experiences not only to the individuals you serve, but to the staff you employ. Kevin talks about improved outcomes like staff retention, mission adherence, and sustainability. Those all are important. But what I like best about this book is that managers, supervisors, administrators, and CEOs — all of you — will be better able to offer and sustain those healing experiences after reading this book. And for that I am grateful.

Lara Palay, LISW-S

## introduction

When I first started compiling the notes, ideas, research, and stories for this book, one of the first file names I used was a question: How do you make it stick? As an outline began to form for what would eventually become this book, that phrase, "making it stick," well, stuck, and it became the real focus. Trauma Responsive Care is about change. And *Making It Stick* was the working title of this book for a long time.

I've been involved in many different efforts to change — from changing personal habits to changing treatment approaches to changing operations in a major division of a Fortune 500 company, and everything in between. I've been obsessed with change. My career has revolved around change, and I even wrote my thesis on change.[1] Over the years, I've learned some important lessons about change. Making a change is hard enough, but making it stick is even harder. And making it stick is the only part that really counts.

I've also learned, as with so many things in life, that change consists of an achieved balance — the balance of planning and constructing, of occupying and maintaining. These pages, for instance, are, from one perspective, about constructing. But more to the point, they are about inhabiting a new place, doing a new thing, moving forward.

In human services, we are, I think, very good at taking on the language of change while impacting what we do as little as possible. This is especially true of training initiatives. We get the training and hope for lasting impact but don't really do anything to make sure the impact actually happens. It seems a perpetual case of "meet the new boss, same as the old boss."[2]

This is somewhat understandable, especially in services to people with intellectual and developmental disabilities. We work within a bifurcated system with a third-party payer that rigidly defines the services and sets the rates. There is little room for or tolerance of creativity in structure or process. As a result, many of the changes we deal with are subtle changes in attitude or perspective. And so, what we usually end up with is a change in the talk while we retain the same old walk.

The process of implementing Trauma Responsive Care is wholly different. It cannot be the same. We must make a profound change and we must make it stick. The purpose of this book is to help with that and to provide a guide to the way forward.

This book, *The Way Forward: Implementing Trauma Responsive Care for Intellectual and Developmental Disability Professionals*, is a companion to Lara Palay's *The Way Through: Trauma Responsive Care for Intellectual and Developmental Disability Professionals*. Both books are forged from almost a decade of working with providers, exploring and developing research-based ways of being truly responsive to trauma, as well as ways to make these new practices an inseparable part of an organization's culture — how it thinks and feels about itself. This has been the bulk of our work together as Aldridge Palay Consulting, and it has been informed by the decades of experience — clinical, organizational, and managerial — each of us brings to the table. Many of the examples used in this book come from our work together.

It is meant, first and foremost, to be a straightforward guide to implementing the values, concepts, and practices Palay presents. It is written primarily for leaders in provider organizations, but its application is much wider than that. It will be useful to anyone seeking to spark change toward a more trauma-responsive approach in an organization, or even a particular division or service site of an organization. It also contains important information for policy-makers and others who seek to influence how supports are provided to people with intellectual and developmental disabilities (I/DD), such as advocates, self-advocates, trainers, and consultants. No matter what your perspective on or place in the I/DD field, you will find, in this book, ways to influence your corner of it toward a more responsive way of interacting with those who are struggling with trauma.

As the basic purpose of this book is to be a practical as opposed to a theoretical guide, I have structured it to serve that purpose. This is, however, a complicated subject. Trauma Responsive Care is steeped in current research in areas like traumatology, attachment theory, and neural sciences. Tying those threads together into an easy-to-understand goal — helping someone feel safe, connected, and in control — and then providing tools to help you do that (the CALMER Skills), as Palay outlined, takes a great deal of research and expertise. *The Way Through*, at its core, seeks to transform a moment — our interaction with the people we support and with each other — into one of empathy, presence, and healing. *The Way Forward* seeks to transform our provider organizations into *producers* of that transformation — *generators* of empathy, presence, and healing. This can only be done by transforming the mechanisms we use to do what we do every day. These mechanisms are things like hiring, training, scheduling, documenting, supervising, and taking corrective action. They are also things like coaching, mentoring, planning, responding to crises, allocating resources, and monitoring and improving quality. These mechanisms find their expression in policies and procedures, management style, and our corporate culture, and it is here where we must plant and nurture change.

Trauma Responsive Care is a "systems" approach, which means the clinical parts, like helping someone feel safe, connected, and in control, are interdependent with operations, things like the structures, the procedures, and the style of an organization, and all are ultimately reflected in policy and culture. This systems approach is necessary to turn isolated moments of connection and healing into the basis for all interactions throughout the organization. Every part of the organization must be influenced, impacted, and changed. Then the change must be made sustainable.

This task requires whole new branches of research and expertise, like systems theory, organizational and industrial psychology, change management, and business and management sciences. And so, this book draws on these fields for a similar purpose, that of managing organizational transformation into a truly trauma-responsive environment, and then providing the guidance and tools to help you meet that goal and help you make it stick. In doing so, I have drawn upon research and upon my own experiences in managing change in this and other industries. I have also woven stories throughout to help codify certain concepts or insights and keep them firmly on the ground, not floating in theory.

As we get started, it will be helpful to understand some of the nuance involved in presenting the materials and to consider some of the challenges I encountered in writing this book and how I resolved them.

The first, I have already mentioned. It is the apparent subtle nature of this change, and it adds some difficulty right from the outset. It will feel, at times, so subtle that you will find it difficult to convey. Like in many things, understanding and communicating a process of change is easier if circumstances are clear — e.g., it's clear we must change because we will go out of business if we don't. As we'll see, part of the challenge of implementing this change is in articulating a sense of urgency around what many might see as an obscure set of impersonal statistics or a minor point of quality improvement. Let's do something about it, sure, but change *everything*? I deal with this problem mostly in Chapter Two, discussing the lessons from research into change management.

Also, I needed to perform a few balancing acts in this book. What level of theoretical, abstract, or general knowledge about management and management theory is necessary, or useful, or interesting? I understand that not everyone shares my love of the abstract and theoretical (a side effect of my study of philosophy, I'm sure). There is, however, some background or more abstract information necessary for context and understanding. I have attempted at every turn to forge this balance. In line with this balance, I have structured the book to revolve around Part Three, which is a step-by-step guide to implementing Trauma Responsive Care. And so, the major themes and insights are presented in the first two parts in a more rounded discussion, and then reviewed in Part Three in a more concise manner.

As a systems approach to managing this change, the content of the various chapters is interconnected and interdependent. As such, there are numerous possible starting points. For example, an endeavor such as this one probably starts with training, whether for a few at a conference or a larger training day for staff. After some training, a deeper interest is ignited, and leadership may then seek ways to make the change stick.

I have opted to anchor these various components with leadership and to start at the decision to transform. This allows me to present the necessary elements of assessing and preparing by senior management to set the stage. It also allows for the tasks and activities to be presented in a sequential way — first this and then that. We know, however, that changes in perception, attitude, and values — changes in our culture — also happen organically and so must be nurtured as opposed to created. This is also why we start with an assessment — to see where you are, what seeds have already been planted, and which parts of this overall process you must emphasize over other parts to complete the change and make it stick.

Another complication arising from a thoroughly interrelated and interdependent system comes in the difficulties of presenting the various levels of detail. I can, for instance, barely introduce the various parts of the organization before I must provide some information about the tasks a given area must perform for it to make sense as you continue reading. So, as you read this book, especially Part Two ("Who Does What and How?"), you will do best to think of them as building on each other. Think of it as riding in a plane to survey the various sections of an area, like a lake, a series of hills, and, say, a woodland. We can only learn so much about each area and how they are arranged with one another by flying in a straight line at the same altitude. Instead, we are going to circle the terrain several times at various altitudes. Each pass reveals a bit more about each part and about the whole area.

As you read this book and start implementing Trauma Responsive Care, the largest barrier you will confront is time. Over many years of working in and with a wide variety of organizations, I have come to see the tension of time is probably the most prevalent barrier to positive change as well as the most powerful ally of organizational entropy.

Various barriers — lack of momentum, waning interest, and other external influences — can all hinder our work in implementing Trauma Responsive Care, but they always seem to get down to this: We just don't have the time. When I talk with organizations about ways to hire high-performing managers, for example, I hear this a lot: "That all sounds great, but we need someone in this seat now — we can't take the time to ..."

It is easy to be flippant about this and simply say you must take the time. But it is a serious matter in organizations, and "just do it" is easier said than done — especially now, given the last few years of a global pandemic and a strange new labor market. But the truth is, this tension is always with us, and time is not really the issue, even though we may experience it that way. In truth, this tension plays itself out in two ways, today vs. tomorrow and management vs. leadership.

Any organization, no matter what it does, must focus first and foremost on today. This is a consistent and effective focus on day-to-day operations and is the "stuff" of management. However, there is a balance to be sought between today and planning for tomorrow, and this planning is the "stuff" of leadership. This balance is also the organizational version of being present — not too distracted by successes or failures of the past and not overly concerned with the future. An organization must dedicate some time and effort to learning from the past. It must also dedicate some time and effort to planning for the future. But just as it must not live in the past, the organization cannot live in the future.

As you read this book, especially in Parts One and Two, you will see this tension expressed in terms of the role of leadership in implementing Trauma Responsive Care and in what we will call the management-leadership paradox. This paradox lies in the fact that the need to balance learning from the past, focusing on current operations, and planning for the future all rest on the managers of an organization. It is that quality in managers we call "leadership" that insists on this balance and insists on forging a path into a new future, into tomorrow, moving forward, even though that may seem to infringe upon or take time away from our focus of today.

The basic thesis of this book, presented in Chapter One, is that, even though we have made great progress, the I/DD community, especially providers of services and supports, still does not pay enough attention to the devastating effects of trauma on the people we support and on one another. And the industry is in desperate need of leaders dedicated to continued progress in this area. You are one of those leaders.

## How to Read This Book

The book is broken down into three parts, with each part focusing on a question. As mentioned, this book is meant to be as practical and concrete as possible while still grappling with the many nuances and barriers to the kind of organizational change we are talking about. This focus starts with the chapter titles themselves, which name the most direct of questions: Why?, Who?, What?, How?, and When? By focusing on these concrete questions, each chapter provides information for the reader as well as material the reader will actually use to implement Trauma Responsive Care.

Chapter One asks why we need to contemplate this change to begin with. It makes the case for this change in terms of the people you support, your workforce, and the overall health of your organization and its business model. The rest of Part One concentrates on change, first on the nature of change in general and lessons from the literature on organizational change (Chapter Two), then on the nature of this change to Trauma Responsive Care itself (Chapter Three).

Part Two then focuses on who does what and how. Chapters Four, Five, and Six are all titled "Who Does What and How?" with each part of the larger question emphasized. As each answer is developed, each component is presented in terms of how it relates to everything else. This systems approach follows a rule of three. Following this rule of three streamlines the implementation of Trauma Responsive Care by creating a system of interlocking and interrelated steps. These steps, eight in all, are presented in Part Three as a guide to implementing Trauma Responsive Care.

The best way to proceed is to read the whole book and then use Part Three as a handbook for the actual implementation and change process. Part One sets a general foundation and so is more abstract. Part Two, while more direct, provides the whole systems approach to Trauma Responsive Care, again, looking at who in the organization is responsible for what and the best ways for all of this to be accomplished, and how to make the change. On this foundation, the more instruction-like guidance of Part Three is much more straightforward. Also, each step in Part Three contains references to Parts One and Two, so you can easily review the forest, if I may use the metaphor, while you are planting a particular tree. The Introduction to Part Three provides more information on this feature.

Another option, of course, is to start with Part Three and use the guidance just mentioned to refer to the parts of the book that deal more fully with that particular subject. Those familiar with the concepts discussed in Parts One and Two may find this more expedient. Still, it is important to carefully read Chapters One and Three.

I have used endnotes to document citations and list other references. I have also, in some cases, used endnotes to expand a discussion or provide additional information that does not warrant space in the main text but adds to the overall content of the book. Naturally, I urge you to read them.

• • •

And so, we are at the beginning of the book and this introduction to it is the last of it to be written. I have come to see that this book is about building something new and making it last.

It's not just a plan or a map. It will help you chart a course to get from point A to point B and provide some tools to help as you stumble along the way. But it also provides the resources for *staying* at point B once you get there. It offers the skills and knowledge you'll need to make the change stick. This is the way forward.

## part one

## Why Change?

> "They that do good to anyone, do also good to themselves; not only in the consequence, but in the very act of doing it; for the conscience of well-doing is an ample reward."
>
> —Seneca[3]

## chapter one

## Why Should an Agency Try to Be Responsive to Trauma?

"I am not bound to win, but I am bound to be true.
 I am not bound to succeed,
  but I am bound to live up to what light I have."

—Abraham Lincoln

On Wednesday, September 23, 1908, it was partly cloudy in upper Manhattan. The temperature was hovering in the low 70s and there was a light breeze. It was the bottom of the ninth and the Chicago Cubs were tied at one apiece with the then-New York Giants; the Giants were at bat.

With two outs, Harry Elwood "Moose" McCormick was on third and rookie Fred Merkle, who had singled down the right-field line was leading off first. Al Bridwell was at the plate. Bridwell connected with his first pitch, a fastball, and whacked what would probably have been a single into center field. The runners vaulted into action. McCormick tagged the plate and the Polo Grounds exploded in cheers as the crowd poured onto the field. Chicago and New York were again neck and neck for the National League pennant, and this was a big win.

Or was it?

Merkle had punched toward second, from instinct as much as anything else, but slowed as what seemed like all of New York crowded in celebration on the field. You've seen it on TV at any given sporting event — the game won, a massive wave of pent-up emotion drives literally thousands of fans onto the field.

And Merkle was right in the middle, slowing his progress to second, bathing in the congratulatory rush of fans, dodging those a little too wound up. He turned toward the Giants' dugout, probably proud he had done his part with a brisk single that set up McCormick's winning run. A Giants pitcher, coaching first base, ended up with the ball and tossed it up for fans to tussle over.

Meanwhile, either Cubs second baseman Johnny Evers or manager/first baseman Frank Chance (exactly which one, along with many of the "facts on the ground" are still up for debate) had seen that Merkle had not tagged second. Evers shouted to outfielder Solly Hofman to retrieve the ball and get it to him at second. Then, with the ball in hand, Evers jumped on the bag, making sure the umpires saw him do it. All this happened in a matter of minutes.

The umpires conferred and made the call. Merkle did not tag his base, so during that final play, a run was scored with a forced out at second. And with a forced out in the play, the scoring run did not count. The game ended tied 1-1. In effect, on that day, the Giants simply didn't finish the game.[4]

I love this story because I'm a Cubs fan and we have to grab glory where we can. The Cubs won the World Series that year and did not equal that feat until 2016, 108 years later, finally snapping the longest dry spell in any sport anywhere. I also like it because it makes me think about the importance of doing everything you can do for the win, for the team, for the greater good, which always starts with simply finishing.

And it is, I think, a perfect analogy for setting the stage for this book and for our field and how we support people with intellectual and developmental disabilities also struggling with trauma. It makes me ask, "Are we finishing the game?"

As we think about that, let's look at the question that started this chapter: "Why should an agency try to be responsive to trauma?" To answer this question, let's look at it from three perspectives, that of supporting the people we serve, our customers; that of supporting the people we employ, our workforce; and that of the effectiveness of our organizations in living our mission and values.

### Trauma Responsive Care: Supporting Our Customers

When I was just starting at the Ohio Department of Developmental Disabilities in 2008, I attended quite a few small conferences and advocacy group meetings. At these conferences, there was usually a plenary session where a group of deputies from various loosely affiliated departments would take turns running through policy priorities or addressing a general topic of interest. It was the beginning of a new administration, and these kinds of sessions occurred frequently through the spring and fall conference season that year. So, we got to know one another. Through these months, I noticed my counterpart in mental health seemed always to talk about trauma.

After some time and a few in-depth conversations, I started to realize that she was like the young preacher who goes to her new church and preaches the same sermon three weeks in a row. When the people confront her about it, asking "Don't you have any other sermons?" she replies, "You'll get the second as soon as you do something about the first."

We are finally catching on. More and more agencies Aldridge Palay works with these days have a basic understanding of trauma.

We are getting, after a slow start, trauma-informed. The trauma-informed agenda is, in some parts of our field, a priority, and many grant funders have built aspects of trauma-informed care into the requirements of their grants. And more approaches are emerging that are explicitly trauma-informed and trauma-responsive. We are making great progress. We are beginning to understand this first question in our inquiry: Why should an agency try to be responsive to trauma in the first place?

There are ample and growing sources of information to answer the question of why this attention on trauma is so important, including Palay's *The Way Through,* which I mentioned earlier.[5] Palay and others[6] have approached this question from a clinical perspective.

As clinicians, these authors are interested in studies and research and sound scientific conclusions. When we add an interest in the organization's ability to fully support its customers and policy's ability to positively impact as many lives as possible, we are reminded that statistics are made up of real people, any one of whom we may support. As a businessperson and a policymaker, I am oriented toward numbers and what those numbers tell us, so this reminder is always welcome.

It is widely accepted that people with disabilities are more susceptible to exposure to trauma and its negative effects.[7] There is ample evidence of this among children with disabilities where we have more robust information. One population-based study, for example, found that children with intellectual disabilities were 2.9 times more likely to have experienced emotional abuse and 3.4 times more likely to have experienced physical abuse than children without an intellectual disability. These children were also 5.3 times more likely to have experienced neglect and an astounding 6.4 times more likely to have experienced sexual abuse.[8] Another study determined that 31% of children with disabilities (25% of this group specifically had I/DD) experienced maltreatment, while only 9% of children without a disability did.[9]

These experiences and the problems they may cause in children and in adults often go unnoticed and untreated for a variety of reasons, not least of which is diagnostic overshadowing, the tendency to ascribe indicators or symptoms of other conditions to the disability itself, thus missing underlying conditions like mental illness or trauma.[10] In light of this, let's widen our scope.

First, let's look at mental health factors. A person with I/DD is two to four times more likely to suffer from a co-occurring mental illness.[11] That's an overall prevalence of mental illness of 41%.[12] Here are a few more stats:

- 30% of people with I/DD have a co-occurring mood disorder.
- 27% have anxiety.
- 28% have a behavioral disorder.
- 54% take a medication usually prescribed for a mental illness.[13]

These diagnoses become more important when you consider that many of them could contain misdiagnosed or undiagnosed trauma.

What's it like for an adult with a disability living in the community? First of all, 26% live in poverty.[14] And that's just the tip of the iceberg.

- 3 of every 1,000 people with a disability have experienced rape or violent sexual assault.
- 36 of every 1,000 experience some other kind of sexual victimization.
- Researchers estimate that only 1 in 30 of these assaults is reported.[15]

From the perspective of any social policy problem up for discussion, from mental health to physical health, from education to employment, from early childhood to elder care, having a disability puts you at high risk of any and all of them.[16]

When you roll all this up, researchers think that anywhere from 60 to 90% of people with I/DD may struggle with trauma.[17]

So, as we look deeper, we learn that people with I/DD are more likely than the general public to suffer from life events we know can cause "Big T" trauma (sexual or physical attack, war, major accidents, natural disasters, etc.). We also know that people with I/DD are more susceptible to "little t" trauma (these are events that are comparatively minor causes of pain, embarrassment, or stress — the damage comes not so much from severity as from frequency).[18] We know the impact of "little t" trauma can be just as significant as that of "Big T" trauma, but we know precious little else. Palay says, "I've never yet seen an instrument that can measure how many times in a day someone feels ignored, misunderstood, devalued, or overwhelmed."[19]

This information can be quite daunting. So, as you think about it, ask yourself this question, "Are we finishing the game?"

Let's take a closer look at that final point: *Anywhere from 60 to 90% of people with disabilities may struggle with trauma.* First of all, I'm sure you would agree, 90% is, for all practical purposes, 100%. Even 60% is striking from a business perspective. Say I'm going to start a lemonade stand and my market research (you know, because everyone who starts a lemonade stand does market research) tells me that 60% of my neighborhood — my whole market — either dislikes, is intolerant of, or is even allergic to lemons. Don't you think I'd change my business model, maybe think about iced tea?

Well, up to 90% of your whole "market" — all your potential customers, the people your mission drives you to support — needs you and your staff, all of them, to understand, empathize with, and be truly responsive to their struggle with trauma. Without this, we are not finishing the game.

**TRAUMA RESPONSIVE CARE: SUPPORTING OUR WORKFORCE**
My mother is a nice lady. You'd like her. She's quick with conversation and can be quite witty. She's active in her church. She starts her day with coffee and ends it with tea and a biscuit (translation: a cookie, usually shortbread). That, and a very slight accent is what might betray her as English. Meeting her, you would never suspect she was exposed to significant, potentially traumatic, life events, but she was. She was a young girl in England during World War II. She lived in Ham, a stone's throw from Richmond, a borough of London.

My mother was evacuated during the so called "Battle of Britain," air attacks on the city by the German air force in the summer and fall of 1940.[20] It was a traumatic time. London was a war zone and Germany was using the newly developed V-1 flying bombs. These primitive missiles would be launched on a trajectory to run out of fuel over London and fall from the sky. My mother recalls the drone of the engines overhead sputtering into silence; she'd then wait for the impact. One time, a sudden gust of wind caused a bomb to just miss the bus she was riding.

The evacuation of London was hastily planned, and each child or family group was assigned a destination and, based on that, a time of departure, a specific train, and a specific car of that train. My mother would occasionally tell stories of those days and her experiences. During one of these times, some fifty years after it happened, she talked specifically about a friend who was on her train. She couldn't recall the girl's name or anything about her after the evacuation, even though they went to the same school. Then suddenly my mother grew silent. At that moment while talking about the events of the trip she remembered, for the first time in five decades, that this little girl had fallen off the train and was killed. She had just recalled it.

This is a fascinating and sad story, but as far as trauma goes, it's not that uncommon. First, a lot of us experience potentially traumatic life events — 70% of us, according to the National Council for Behavioral Health.[21] And research suggests that as many as 32% of us who have been exposed to trauma experience what is called "delayed recall" of those traumatic events, just as my mother had.[22] And this is just "Big T" trauma.

Now at this point we could extrapolate that about 70% of our potential workforce has been exposed to trauma (though some may not even know it). Does that mean that 70% of our workforce struggles with trauma? Not necessarily. There are many different factors that play into one's susceptibility to suffering trauma-related symptoms once exposed. And, obviously more exposure increases the chances of suffering from symptoms. Even though this number of 70% prevalence of exposure does not directly translate into having trauma, this figure does present a benchmark for us as we take a closer look at our workforce.

The other benchmark researchers can get at with relative confidence is the gathering of symptoms and severity of symptoms that make up the diagnosis of Post-Traumatic Stress Disorder (PTSD). In other words, if 70% of us are exposed, how many are significantly impacted? The answer: about 7%. Overall, the National Institute of Mental Health reckons the prevalence of PTSD is 3.6% annually with a lifetime prevalence of 6.8%.[23]

We can think of these two markers, 70% exposure to trauma and 7% significant impact from it, as sitting at either end of a spectrum. What about delayed recall? What about traumatic stress and related symptoms? What about the various effects of burnout, anxiety, the stress of poverty, the stress of a pandemic? What about all the trauma-related stuff that is either under or untreated, or misdiagnosed? All this is between our two benchmarks — 70% exposure and 7% known negative impact — in a great, big gray area.

As a result, when we think about the general population (much like when we discuss the people we support), in terms of trauma, there is a great deal we do not know. Some of this, to quote former U.S. Secretary of Defense Donald Rumsfeld, includes "known unknowns," things we know happen but we can't very easily get at, like estimates of undiagnosed or missed cases of PTSD or the known impact of "little t" trauma we can't really quantify. And some of it, as we saw earlier, we just don't know.

Here's what we do know: The workforce we draw from is not exactly the general population. Our typical Direct Support Professional is a woman (about 71%), in her mid-40s with a high school education and maybe some or all of a two-year degree (50%). She is probably white (nationally about 68% white and 32% people of color), but we are drawing significantly from minorities and people new to the United States.[24] This typical member of our workforce is also quite similar to nurse aides, home healthcare workers, and childcare workers. But the keyword in this paragraph is *women*. Overwhelmingly, we depend on women to do the work of our organizations. And that work, not to put too fine a point on it, is low-paying healthcare work.

These numbers, these statistics, are made up of real people, like my mother. When I started in this field, she fell right in the middle of the most significant demographic of our workforce. And, although she did not develop PTSD, whether she had or not, no job application would catch her experiences as a child and her delayed recall of a traumatic experience.

Women are known to be two to three times more likely than men to develop PTSD. In fact, over a lifetime, the prevalence of PTSD in women is 10% to 12%, while it is only 5% to 6% in men. Women are less likely than men to be exposed to trauma generally, but more likely than men to be exposed to the kinds of trauma most likely to lead to PTSD, like sexual abuse and attacks.[25,26]

Working in healthcare, especially in the midst of a pandemic, can also mean higher likelihood of struggling with trauma. A recent systematic review from 2016, before the pandemic, looking at nine studies, found a PTSD prevalence of 14.8%[27] among healthcare workers. This review, admittedly, focused on physicians. But a meta-analysis from 2020, looking at 117 studies, found in healthcare workers an elevated prevalence of PTSD of 13%.[28] This meta-analysis also identified factors linked to the increased likelihood of developing these and other conditions. One of these factors is being a woman.[29]

Add to this the known correlation between low income and toxic stress,[30] and you can begin to see where our organizations lie regarding trauma. And all these stressors — low pay, inadequate training, and burnout — impact work attitude, perspectives, and practices.[31]

We draw from a workforce with a better-than-average chance of exposure to trauma and a better-than-average chance of that exposure negatively impacting their lives. And we draw on this workforce to support people with exposure rates to trauma possibly as high as 90%.

And with all this, what did this workforce do in the face of a global pandemic that traumatized governments and Fortune 500 companies alike? They stepped up.

- 90% had access to and used personal protective equipment; 27% even used homemade masks.
- 44% worked additional hours.
- 35% worked different shifts and 28% worked at additional sites.
- 43% took on additional duties and responsibilities.

All this for an average wage of $13.92 — and 70% did not get any bonus or jump in pay for stepping up.[32]

If we were in manufacturing, the work — and the budget — of maintaining the machinery would be top priority, mission-critical. Our workforce *is* the machinery of what we do in any human services arena. If we are not doing everything possible to provide our Direct Support Professionals (DSPs) with everything they need, including and especially a management team that is responsive — truly responsive — to the high levels of trauma exposure in our workforce, how can we be living out our mission?

The truth is we can't. If we don't come face to face with the epidemic levels of trauma in our workforce, then we are not finishing the game.

## Trauma Responsive Care:
## Supporting Our Organizations

The organizational or business case for implementing Trauma Responsive Care is quite simple: Trauma Responsive Care creates alignment. It helps us systematically align:

• Mission and values with customer needs
• Customer needs with our value proposition
• Our value proposition with demonstrated values

And all that is based on aligning staff capacity for responsiveness to trauma.

If, in the first place, your product or service doesn't align with your customer's need, you are going to lose the game. This is the case for supporting our customers. In the second place, if your staff members are ill-equipped to meet the needs of your customers, or they work to do so in spite of management instead of with the support of management, you'll struggle to stay in the game. This is the case for supporting our workforce.

The people our organizations support need to feel, as Trauma Responsive Care puts it, safe, connected, and in control. This is accomplished by aligning staff to help them feel the same. In turn, we know that our staff, showing up for their shift, need to feel safe, connected, and in control. This is accomplished by aligning management to help them feel that way. This alignment is, in a nutshell, what this entire book is about.

Creating business-model alignment is best visualized as a square, with four distinct sides (see Figure 1.1).[33] This is also helpful in making the business case for Trauma Responsive Care.

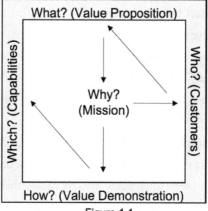

Figure 1.1

In the center is our mission — "Why do we do what we do? What is the purpose of the organization's existence?" No matter what words we use, it must finally boil down to providing support to this particular population of people — people with intellectual and developmental disabilities.

This gets us to the right side of the square: our customers. In particular, we are concerned with the overwhelming exposure to trauma that so clearly defines our customers. As we have already established, supporting people with I/DD means supporting people with trauma. Struggling with trauma is not a choice or preference expressed by our customers, it is a basic characteristic of how they encounter their environment.

When we move to the top of the square, the question is, "What is our value proposition? What value do we offer our customers?" As struggling with trauma is a basic characteristic of our customer, any value proposition worth anything has to take this into account. If our value proposition does not, at its core, include responsiveness to trauma, we are, by definition, out of alignment. As a result, we cannot, no matter what else we get right, provide the best support for the people we serve.

On the bottom of the square, the question is, "How do we demonstrate this value?" Again, alignment requires that this demonstration of the value proposition contains, at its core, responsiveness to trauma.

Finally, on the left side — "What capacities are needed to continually demonstrate the value proposition we offer the customer?" This side of the alignment square gets directly at whether or not things like management style or staff skills are responsive to trauma and whether the actions of staff in each emerging moment, supporting the people they support, are responsive to trauma.

I want to be as clear as I can. Our vocation, and the vocation of all our underpaid, underappreciated Direct Support Professionals, is to support people with I/DD. People with I/DD are traumatized — at astounding levels. If what we do, whatever it is, with them, in support of them, for them, is not responsive to their trauma, then we are failing our mission before we even start.

If we're not going to tag second, what's the point of leaving first?

## WHY SHOULD AN AGENCY TRY TO BE RESPONSIVE TO TRAUMA?

This book is a series of questions, and this first question has been "Why?" "Why should we be responsive to trauma?" I've shown the need for responsiveness on the part of the customer, and I've shown the need for responsiveness on the part of our workforce. And I've shown how all this demands that we align this responsiveness through our mission and operations if we are going to actually live out our mission.

Trauma Responsive Care provides this alignment, but implementing Trauma Responsive Care and gaining this thorough alignment in our organizations requires change. And change is difficult. For the rest of Part One, we are going to concentrate on change. First, we'll look at managing change generally (Chapter Two), and then we'll look at *this* change specifically (Chapter Three). Then, in Part Two, we'll ask the next questions: "Who does what and how?"

## The Nature of Change

"The sun is new every day."

—Heraclitus[34]

There is an old naval story that's been floating around in some form or another since the early twentieth century. It goes something like this:

There is a ship on maneuvers in choppy seas with a dense fog. Observation sees a faint light in the distance, so the captain orders the radio operator to make contact and direct the oncoming vessel to turn fifteen degrees north to avoid collision. This, the radio operator does:

SHIP: "This is the USS Abraham Lincoln to unidentified vessel. Please turn fifteen degrees north... "

RESPONSE: "Suggest you turn fifteen degrees south to avoid collision."

SHIP: "Negative. I say again, change your course fifteen degrees north."

RESPONSE: "You change *your* course. Fifteen degrees south."

At this point, the captain is getting more and more irate and jumps on the radio himself.

CAPTAIN: "This is the aircraft carrier USS Abraham Lincoln of the United States Navy, the biggest carrier in the Atlantic Fleet. You *will* change your course fifteen degrees north or we will take necessary action to protect this ship and her mission!"

RESPONSE: "Well, we're a lighthouse, so, your call."

This story is not true, although the United States Navy has been nagged by it for decades.[35] It is a story about the need to be open to new ideas, even when your course is set. It is a story about the various events that come up that cause us to divert our direction in life, whether we want to change or not.[36]

There are some deeper elements of change in the story that sometimes go unnoticed. The story is a narrative; it has a beginning and a middle, and regardless of what the captain decides to do, it will end — it progresses. Time goes by, and so does everything else. There is an increased tension from the ship, partly because in the two- or three-minute exchange, the ship is now two or three minutes closer to a collision. Change is endemic; change happens.

This story and our work are like the quote at the start of this chapter. The sun is new every day. Everything is constantly changing.

Our organizations are constantly changing. Today is not the same as yesterday, and next month will not be the same as this month, even though we try to smooth everything out. And on top of the regular flow of events, things happen, and we need to change quickly, whether we planned for it or not. Other times, we may see things approaching and have time for a little advanced preparation and planning. This is a basic fact of organizational life: You have to change course, because the lighthouse won't.

It is also this basic fact of change that delivers the events and the shifting economic, regulatory, or knowledge-based circumstances to which our organizations have to respond.

So, what is change? Or, more concretely, what does change look like in the life of our agencies, particularly as we are thinking of this change to Trauma Responsive Care? We're going to build a deeper understanding of this process by first looking at some of the characteristics of change that may feel more familiar to us. Then we'll look at the tasks and pitfalls involved in managing change. In doing so, I hope to spend just enough time on the forest to find our tree.

## CONTENT AND CONTEXT

When I taught graduate students at the Ohio State University College of Social Work, I sometimes taught a class called Organizational and Community Change. I routinely started with a discussion on the emergence of discontentment and how individuals experience a problem and eventually talk to one another. In this way, the community slowly realizes there's a problem. At some point, the status quo, or the *is*, becomes increasingly unsatisfying. This discontent becomes fertile ground for a new vision, an *ought*. The statement, "It is like this" becomes, "It shouldn't be like this." This change opens the door to "It *ought* to be like this." In other words, this recognition of discontentment, that things could be better, places change in a necessary context.

In social work practice, when dealing with organizational or community change, it's best to start with helping the organization or community define the problem. In this way, the process of change always has three concrete elements — and conveniently, they all start with the letter *P*: The context for change is based on the

problem, the people, and the place. You have to start by defining the
Problem with the People it impacts, in the Place where it impacts
them. This, in turn, allows for the larger stakeholder and political
context to come into sharper focus (see Figure 2.1).[37]

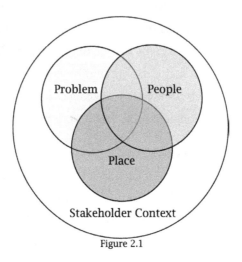

Figure 2.1

This perspective of content and context helps us connect the
problem with the need for change and then both of these to the
people the problem and the proposed solution impacts. And that
keeps us focused.

From a business perspective, this focus can be more easily kept,
as business naturally centers around a few key metrics. What would
cause us to create change in our business? There are many possibilities, like erosion in profitability or market share or a loss of competitiveness, key patents ending or products becoming outdated, or
pending technological advancements.[38] And these can all impact
our businesses as providers of services to people with I/DD. But
we also serve our mission and so, as we talk more about change, an

initial focus on the connection between the problem we are trying to solve and the people impacted right where they live is important.

In Trauma Responsive Care, we recognize we have not been supporting our mission as well as we could be — we have not done as well by our customers as we could have (see Chapter One).

In short, we are making this change because the clinical, social, and business context in which we operate make it necessary if we are to fully align ourselves with our mission to support people with intellectual and developmental disabilities to the best of our ability.

### Scope and Intensity

Everything we do or any changes we make, as individuals or in organizations, follows the same course as any narrative or story: It has a beginning, a middle, and an end. And in the middle is the change itself. You do something so your location, your direction, or the thing you're doing, changes — something is markedly different at the end as compared to the beginning. Some changes are relatively straightforward, like changing a form. Then it's as simple as this: On Friday we were using the old form, and on Monday we are using the new form. But some changes are a bit more complicated, so what will be markedly different at the end takes a bit more time and thought to define, and it requires commitment to complete. We can understand this better by thinking of any change in terms of its scope and intensity.

Think of the scope of change in the organization as how widespread the change is. Or another perspective is, how many people or divisions are impacted? The intensity of the change is how much — how much will this change impact a given person's job or a division's functioning? Allow me to illustrate.

I once had the privilege of working as the chief executive of a wholly owned subsidiary, one of several companies under single ownership. During my time with the organization, all the companies underwent a change in legal status from an S corporation status to a limited liability company (LLC) status. Also during my tenure, there were some significant changes in regulatory oversight around the tracking and reporting of incidents in my state. We also, at that time, planned for and transitioned to a phone-based timekeeping and billing system, customized to meet the variety of circumstances of each service provided by each company, across the country. All three of these were changes deemed necessary by leadership to stay viable and competitive in the marketplace and to position ourselves to better serve our customers. As we think about these three processes and the scope and intensity of each one, our understanding of and appreciation for the elements of change in each process deepens.

With the first, you can imagine senior management were very much involved, checking and double-checking documents, conferring with legal counsel and putting other changes into motion, like business cards and letterhead. You can imagine that legal counsel, handling ten or twelve of these changes in as many different states, were also very busy, dealing with differing requirements of registration, notification, and approval. The intensity of this change for the people mentioned was high. But for the vast majority of my 300-plus employees, this change had very little impact, and their involvement in it was practically nil. The actual number of people who were impacted was rather narrow. So, this change was low in scope but high in intensity (see *Legal Status* in Figure 2.2).

In the second process, managers were involved with support staff in reviewing and understanding the changes in regulations and in building new capacity in gathering and analyzing incident reports. The changes to the incident reports already in use were minimal and easily trained for. In this case, we can see the scope of the impact was much more widespread than the first — just about everyone was impacted. But the level of intensity, while it varied widely, was generally pretty low (see *Reg Changes* in Figure 2.2).

In the third example of transitioning to a phone-based time and billing system, you can imagine intense preparation and planning involving every level of management, significant training requirement, and massive changes to day-to-day, if not hour-by-hour, operations — involving and impacting everyone — high scope and high intensity (see *Timekeeping* in Figure 2.2).

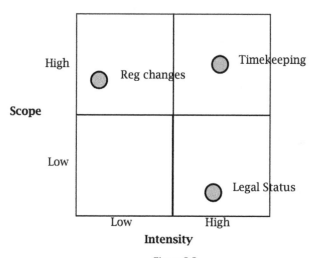

Figure 2.2

As you might guess, in comparison to these instances of change, Trauma Responsive Care is monumental. It will impact everything. It involves training everyone — but it's not just a training initiative. You may not change your mission, but you will have to reinterpret it. You may not need many new policies, but you will have to review all your policies to ensure thorough alignment.[39]

The reason this change is so monumental lies in what kind of change needs to take place. In our illustration of the changes in legal structure, very few people cared if one paycheck said "Inc." and the next one said "LLC," as long as the bank didn't care. In the change to a phone-based timekeeping system, we had to impact every staff member's behavior. Even then, it didn't much matter if the staff liked phones, hated phones, or preferred purple phones, as long as they liked getting paid more. But in moving to Trauma Responsive Care, as we will cover in the next chapter, we also seek to change attitudes, perceptions, and feelings. That makes this kind of change very difficult — high scope and high intensity (see Figure 2.3).[40]

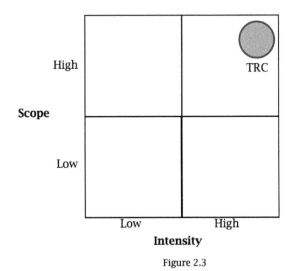

Figure 2.3

## CRISIS VS. STRATEGIC RESPONSE

In our final perspective on change, we can look at change that comes from a response to a crisis or change that comes as a strategic response. We'll see below, when we discuss the stages of managing change, that whether in response to a crisis or as a strategic move, we still need to plan.

We've seen some examples of changes as strategic response above. The perfect example of change as a response to crisis for all of us — and by all, I mean, you know, *all* — were the changes required by the coronavirus pandemic. Because of COVID-19, we changed procurement (both what we bought and how much), we changed training, we changed staffing patterns (all the time), and we changed guidelines for community outings and visitation. We adapted management practices and styles, sometimes on the fly and haphazardly. We struggled with old regulations, responded to new regulations, and tried to keep track of temporary suspensions of regulations. And we learned to deal with other aftershock crises, such as labor shortages.[41] We usually planned rapidly, knowing we'd better circle back sooner rather than later to review and revise.

To help us with the distinction we seek, we can rely on the Eisenhower Decision-Making Matrix (see Figure 2.4). The matrix is made up of four sections that help us think about how to respond when our variables (high or low urgency and high or low importance) converge. If something is both highly important and highly urgent, we have to do it and we have to do it now, so this square is marked "Do." This is the proverbial fire that has to be put out. Something that is highly urgent but of low importance has to be done, but we have some leeway and so we mark it as "Plan" — definitely high on the to-do list, after the proverbial fire is contained. On the other hand, something that is highly important but not that urgent we may "delegate" in terms of when we do it or in terms of who does it — we may outsource this necessary but not mission-critical function. Finally, if we find something to be of low importance and is not at all urgent, we may want to question whether we spend any time on it at all. Though this is an imperfect instrument, it is helpful in gaining some insight into assessing and prioritizing action.

When we think about what we've been through as a field and place it on the Eisenhower Matrix of *important vs. urgent*, we know exactly where all the COVID-related actions and planning fall (see Figure 2.4). COVID planning was both very important — it needed to be done — and very urgent — it needed to be done immediately. If, on the other hand, you were planning something like a transition to a higher level of technology as part of a long-term strategic plan, you might label this as important but not urgent. In the middle of a global pandemic, you might delay that change. As a crisis response, our COVID planning and subsequent changes started and stayed in that top right-hand quadrant.

**COVID Crisis Planning**

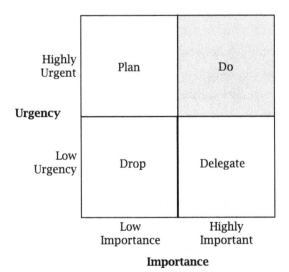

Figure 2.4

Trauma Responsive Care is also both important and urgent. But Trauma Responsive Care is a strategic response, so thorough planning is emphasized. Don't delay it, don't drop it, and don't rush it. You have to be in it for the long haul. As a strategic response and not a response to crisis, Trauma Responsive Care takes up the whole top row of the matrix (see Figure 2.5).

**TRC Strategic Planning**

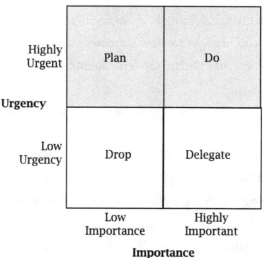

Figure 2.5

### MANAGING CHANGE

Now let's narrow our focus just a bit and talk about change management. What is *change management*? It is coordinating the activities within an organization to successfully navigate the various obstacles and orchestrate various opportunities within the change process toward a specific end. This whole book is on change management, specifically implementing Trauma Responsive Care. So, before we take our next step and look specifically at Trauma Responsive

Care, it might be helpful to look at some of the literature on change management.

We have already talked about why an organization might face change or decide to change. We've also looked at some of the important characteristics of change itself, at least in terms of our task. One of the things we talked about was the fact that change is a story with a beginning, middle, and end. What we're looking for are the plot points along the arc of the story. What are the major steps in creating sustainable change in an organization? As we look at the steps, we'll also begin to see how these steps open into a broader outline. A basic and generic top-level outline would include the following:

- **Defining the problem:** Why do we want to (or have to) change? What are we changing to?
- **Analyzing the change:** What does the change mean; what is its context? What is the scope and intensity of this change?
- **Designing the change:** What's our plan? What do we do first? Second? How does it all tie together?
- **Implementing the change:** Who does what part of the action plan? How will we review and track the change?
- **Assessing the change:** Did we do what we wanted to do? Did we actually change, and are we realizing the intended outcomes?

If you go back and take a quick look at the table of contents, you'll be able to identify the various parts of this basic outline. But what is most useful to us here, and in the change management literature, are the pitfalls — the stuff that could go wrong.

The study of management and managing over the past few decades has been dominated by case studies and what might be called "natural experiments." These case studies are also the building blocks of management education. A natural experiment is where natural events create opportunities to run experiments backward, in a way. Here's a classic example: In 1992, two economists, Lawrence Katz and Allan Krueger, studying the impact of minimum wage on prices, noticed that New Jersey hiked its minimum wage while Pennsylvania did not.[42] They realized by looking at prices in the two states before and after New Jersey's rise, they could decipher the impact of the wage hike. The variable (New Jersey's wage hike) was placed for them in the real world, so they took advantage of the "experiment" by looking at what happened before and after.

In the study of management, Tom Peters and Bob Waterman took a similar approach in their seminal work, *In Search of Excellence*. In essence, they went backward. In trying to figure out what a company had to do to become excellent — top of their industry — they first defined excellence. They developed a list of six empirical measures of top-performing companies. Having identified the top performers among their total sample, they could look at what top performers did that underperformers did not do and could abstract "lessons from America's best-run companies."[43]

Following suit, many of the insights about change in the literature come in the form of lessons from observing change — what worked and what didn't work. The best, most important lessons that emerge can be stated both positively and negatively with equal force and validity. That is, I can say, "You explicitly increase your chance of success if you do X," *and* I can say, "You explicitly decrease your chance of success if you don't do X," and both are true. These double-edged lessons are the essentials, so we will concentrate our time on them.

Work like this obviously contains some measure of abstraction and subjective judgment. Any organization embarking on change, even with some observable commonalities, is its own unique blend of history, personality, culture, and commitment. Using the double criteria of "doing it helps and not doing it hurts" gives these lessons added weight. Further, in gathering these lessons, I have concentrated my attention on those suited for human service organizations, specifically organizations that are mission-driven and dependent on human-to-human interaction, like disability services, implementing Trauma Responsive Care.

Finally, you know your organization best. So, this approach allows you to better judge the relative importance of any and all of the lessons. I will say, however, while you don't have to pay attention to these things, based on the research and on my experiences in the field, you should have a pretty strong reason why you don't.

### Lesson One: Communicate

Communication is essential. Its importance cannot be overstated. It is part of every other lesson. I could resort to platitudes, like *communication is everything*, which I guess I just did. And I can give dictums — *Communication is the circulatory system of the organization* — which I will in Chapter Four. Communication between team members working on aspects of implementing Trauma Responsive Care is vital. Constantly communicating the values of Trauma Responsive Care and telling stories of success and discussing how something worked or didn't work is absolutely vital. In fact, one group of researchers has outlined four phases of leadership communication necessary for a persuasive campaign for change consisting of specific, planned steps, like setting the stage, framing the change plan, managing the mood, and preventing back-sliding.[44] Leaders who tell us what's going to happen and then tell us what's happening, and then tell us what just happened, while also reminding us of why we're doing it and how much better things will be, can truly lead through change.

All of this is true and useful, and we know it, and we all agree — but it's also easily forgotten, overlooked, or just lost. How can we actually remember these known lessons on communication? How can you actually build them into your culture? What can I say or do that would actually help?

What if I slid my desk to within, say, just under twenty feet of yours and told you all that again? Would that help make it stick? Actually, yes, it would help — a lot.

During the Cold War, the U.S. government became interested in efficiency, given all the stuff we were trying to do faster and better than our friends in the Soviet Union. So, in his own little natural experiment, Thomas Allen from MIT started looking at different engineering firms that had solved the same or very similar problems and he compared the quality of the various solutions and then identified practices of the groups with the "best" solutions.[45] What emerged most forcefully was the presence of what Allen called a cluster of high communicators, a group of individuals who communicated a lot and very quickly — insights, findings, theories, calculations. Then he set out to find why these people, these clusters, clustered in the first place. He looked at everything from schools they attended and what they did on their time off, like hobbies or the kinds of books they read, and he found only one factor held in common that actually made a significant difference — proximity. Allen discovered what is now called the Allen Curve. If you separate people by fifty meters (about half a football field), communication virtually stops. This is the email announcement/newsletter zone. Get people within six meters (about nineteen and a half feet), and communication frequency goes through the roof. Each knows what the others are having for lunch. Proximity produces clusters of high communicators, and communication is essential to any change process. In our industry, with multiple service sites and managers always on the go, and with the rise of teleconferencing, replicating proximity can be difficult, but it is possible, and the impact can be vital.

I once worked with an organization that had two teams whose work, though quite different, was interdependent. They needed each other to do their work well, but the two teams were constantly faced with challenges to working well together. The relationship had deteriorated so much that the two divisions saw each other as outsiders to the work of the whole organization. This was one of many factors that led to significant turnover. While still trying to figure out how to avoid these same conflicts as the teams were rebuilding, leadership decided to move the teams closer together (they were in separate buildings on the same campus). The groups started to communicate just because they were closer to each other. "We still have problems," one manager observed, "but now, they don't fester and a lot of them get solved."

### Lesson Two: Build a Sense of Urgency
Developing and communicating a sense of urgency is very important to a successful change effort. There is a certain resistance to change built into every organizational culture that is a necessary part of overall sustainability and viability. That resistance must be

overcome. It's part of what might be called the management/leadership paradox. Management, says John Kotter, of Harvard Business School, has a mandate "to minimize risk and to keep the current system operating. Change, by definition, requires creating a new system, which in turn demands leadership."[46]

Precisely because of this built-in resistance, leadership must create a strong sense of urgency. And because change largely depends on people in the organization understanding a future clearly differentiated from the past, some researchers have emphasized the importance of this sense of urgency over the other lessons presented here.[47]

This approach works well in the kind of change that dominates change management thinking, like eroding margins or negative change in market share, where communicating projections on sales, cost, or market share with and without basic changes may suffice. A plummeting arrow on a line graph marked, "This is where you lose your job unless we do something," can really focus the mind.

But our efforts are more subtle. Becoming responsive to trauma is a value-based decision. It is not about surviving; it is about doing the best we can for the people we support. Your staff must be convinced that becoming actively responsive to trauma and traumatic stress is essential to living out the mission and providing the best supports we can offer. So, developing a sense of urgency is a more delicate task. And leading people to this conclusion through training, discussion, and persuasion — guiding people through the process and, in so doing, building commitment and motivation from the outset — is a more fitting approach.[48] This sense of urgency grows when we talk about how to become and remain part of the healing process for someone struggling with trauma — and how we stop being a barrier to that healing.

### *Lesson Three: Create a Vision*

Let's try a little SAT question:[49]

> "Creating a sense of urgency" is to "defining the problem"
>
> as
>
> "Creating a vision" is to "_____ the problem."

If you said "solving," you are absolutely correct. It is not the solution, but it is the vision of the solution. And, more particularly, it is the vision of the future once the solution has been applied.

When you meet with a builder about building a new house, does the builder brag about new composite siding and show you tensile-strength stats? Eventually they might, but first, they're going to show you pictures of a warm and happy family (preferably with a dog) sitting in front of a fireplace while it snows like crazy outside the window. They are going to give you a vision of the future with you in your new house. That's what you have to do. No dog necessary.

This much has to be made simple and clear. Everyone must see in the vision a future that is markedly different than the past and present. These differences must be clear and must be easy to explain and communicate. It is important to craft this vision and communicate it widely. When you are in the thick of it and the work gets hard and the changes start to cause friction, the vision is the unifying factor, the expression of passion, and the rallying point. Without it, the managers who don't get it or the division head that just doesn't support it will win the day.

There's a guy walking down the street and he sees two bricklayers working about fifty feet apart. He asks the first one, "Hey, what are you doing?" The first one looks at our guy like he's lost or something and says, "I'm laying bricks." Our guy moves on to the next bricklayer and asks the same question. This one swings around, obviously excited, and says, "I'm building a cathedral!"

Be the second one.

### Lesson Four: Rely on Persuasion

Many change efforts start with a realization at the top that there is a need for change followed by programs designed to make the change. These can include training drives, incentive programs, new management targets, new outcome measures, and new job descriptions. I once heard of a change effort on trauma that was simply creating a position for a trauma specialist and then hiring someone. Presumably that person would then figure it all out and ...

This approach doesn't work for most change efforts[50] and it definitely doesn't work with Trauma Responsive Care. The change here is not one of increased skill acquisition alone. That is part of it — and a necessary part for large-scale, easy-to-communicate change. But the change we are really seeking is a change to our organizational culture.

Our culture is the myriad connections between our various perceptions, attitudes, and values, emerging from the unique social and psychological environment of our organization, along with its behavior, operations, and decision-making. This is not something you can change with a few well-placed dictums from the executive suite or a series of trainings. Our organizations are living, breathing things, and change requires discussing, convincing, persuading — and then pulling together.

These emerging interactional influences that make up our organizational culture also affect how the organization sees itself, as well as how it learns and cares and acts. We want this culture, its values, actions, and how it sees itself, to be focused on everyone feeling safe, connected, and in control. So we cannot afford to ignore it, as we tend to do in human services.[51] Again, this alignment takes persuasion.

### Lesson Five: Nurture Change Where It Grows (Instead of Worrying about Where It Isn't Growing)

In baseball, there's a saying: Everybody's going to win fifty-four games and everybody's going to lose fifty-four games. It's what you do with the other fifty-four games that count.[52] When you rely on persuasion, your powers of persuasion will work better on some than others. In all change efforts, some will get on board quickly, and some will be resistant to the end. It's what you do with the rest that counts.

This means you have to be ready for and be open to change taking root and flourishing in some parts of the organization and not in other parts. This is fine, because this is how it happens. Like a garden, change grows unevenly, and you will be tempted to worry about the parts that aren't growing — the managers who aren't "getting it" or the division head that is simply not supporting it. Don't. Nurture the plants that are growing. Celebrate the wins and support the areas, the managers, and the people who *do* get it and are trying to build new habits. That remnant will become the engine of change if nurtured. And later, when institutionalizing the change through new hiring and training practices, new outcome measures, new standards of practice, and new management styles, the change will be as much in the soil as in the individual plants. The garden will thrive.

## *Lesson Six: Grab Short-Term Wins and Leverage Them*

In one engagement, we walked into the offices of a rather large provider for the second of three discussions with managers of one of this agency's regions. Before the meeting started, two managers approached us, excited to tell us a story. One of them had to meet with an employee who, as they described him, was someone who "just shouldn't be working with people." He seemed to be angry all the time and was known to be a bit volatile and had recently acted in ways that required his termination. They were meeting so they could fire him. This was the kind of meeting, one of them said, where you have another manager in the room, give the office staff a heads-up, and sit closest to the door. They decided to "give this Trauma Responsive Care thing a try," so the two managers met before the meeting and went through the CALMER Skills.[53] They discussed how they might help this person they were about to fire feel safe, connected, and in control. Then they went into the meeting to do the deed. The managers told us, "Not only was he calm the whole time, because we remained calm, at the end of the meeting, with termination papers in hand, he thanked us for the opportunity to work for us."

Here's another story. At the beginning of the second visit to a different large agency, a month after Aldridge Palay came in to do a big training, the CEO started a meeting with this anecdote. "I was, I have to say, a bit skeptical," he said, "but the training was interesting — at least the part I could sit in on was. I had to leave for another in a series of highly contentious phone meetings with the head of another agency. As I sat there waiting for the call, I thumbed through the Trauma Responsive Care manual, looking at some of the strategies around the CALMER Skills, and thought, 'Why not?'

When the call started, I tried to practice a few of the strategies. That was the most productive meeting I had ever had with that agency, and the only thing that changed was my attitude going into it."

Stories like these will emerge. People will have these kinds of experiences. And as a leader, you can reinforce the change by telling and retelling these stories of success. Tell them far and wide; better yet, invite the person who told you the story to tell others. Hold meetings just so these stories can be told. You must grab these early wins and use them.

Now let me take things a step further. This is not baseball; we fix games here. If you don't have wins to celebrate — make them! If you do have wins to celebrate — make more! Let's try a little thought experiment. What if the two managers from the first story came to you as their boss and told you they were about to fire Mr. Angry. What if you suggested they try something? "Before you go in there," you tell them, "review the CALMER Skills we just learned; talk about how to make even someone like Mr. Angry feel safe, connected, and in control. Do that and let's see what happens." The fix is in, and the story could be even more potent. Don't make things up, just make things happen.

Find these wins and leverage them.

### Lesson Seven: Institutionalize the Change

For my money, this is the most important part of solidifying long-term change, and as you see, it comes late in the list. Institutionalizing the change brings in what I call the "hard" side of the organization — the stuff you can touch. And I mean this literally; it's all the things you can actually pick up and hand to someone. I'll develop this more in Part Two.

This lesson of institutionalizing refers to the programmatic changes you avoid at the beginning and start to implement later in the project. These are changes to the mission statement or value statements. It also includes changes to policies and procedures, training materials, and, perhaps, job descriptions, incentive programs, and pay structures. All this comes late in the process, but, as we shall see, this process is started right at the beginning.

The reason this lesson is so important is that the written part of the organization is its hard-wired institutional memory. If you don't ground the change in mission, in policies, in board minutes and decisions, then change becomes the previous leader's interest at best, folly at worst. Keep in mind that in most industries and in most organizations, the top and the bottom of the org chart are generally more fluid and experience more changes than the middle of the chart.

I have seen agencies jump in with both feet and make great progress, but with changes in leadership and nothing set in stone, it all evaporated. This lesson of institutionalizing the change is the process of setting it in stone.

### Lesson Eight: Evaluate Continually

This last lesson has to do with vigilance. What do you do at the end? There *is* an end, probably marked by completing the tasks of institutionalizing, but through the latter half, and into the future, leaders have to, paraphrasing the slogan of the Civil Rights Movement, "Keep their eyes on the prize."

Most pressing is data. As you identify both outputs and outcomes and design ways to measure them, you will have to test and tweak these measures to make sure the data is really telling you what you think it's telling you.

And there are plenty of longer-term things to be vigilant about. For example, some opportunities and necessities may emerge in the process to make significant changes in key positions, to the structure of the organization, or to management style. These things can take on their own lives as different processes and must not be allowed to overshadow the real purpose.

And so, we end this quite limited list of lessons of change management where we started the chapter. Change is part of life and part of work. Training materials need to be updated. Key personnel — champions for Trauma Responsive Care — will change jobs or retire. New values, expressed in what we do in these situations, will provide some guidance, but the passion must be kept alive. Though it may start in different places, ultimately, it becomes the role of leadership.

Earlier, I noted that part of building the sense of urgency is creating, for all customers, staff, and stakeholders, a clear vision that is markedly different from the past. This new vision must be seen in leadership.

These lessons serve as a foundation for the rest of the book. And I will identify, especially in Part Three, which of these lessons apply to the various concrete actions you will take to implement Trauma Responsive Care. Now, in the next chapter, let's look at exactly what we are implementing.

chapter three

## The Nature of *This* Change

"As Autumn sweeps the grove's green pride away,
  The new leaves budding as the old decay,
  So, words which flaunt their time in vernal bloom
  Must fall, and fresh ones flourish in their room."

—Horace[54]

After a series of airline disasters through the 1970s, caused by a couple of common issues that fell under the category of human error, NASA convened a conference that would end up developing what is known in aviation as CRM training. CRM stands for Crew Resource Management.

In one of these disasters, the entire flight crew was preoccupied by what was probably a faulty indicator light. During the discussions, investigators concluded, the autopilot was inadvertently disengaged. The plane, over an extended period of time, flew itself into the ground.[55] The crew did not notice the fall in altitude until it was too late. In another, garbled communications and concerns expressed by the first officer but then dismissed by the captain played a significant role in a collision during take-off.[56] In a third incident, the airplane literally ran out of fuel as the crew debated a faulty indicator.[57]

In all these cases, tried-and-true flight crews, in state-of-the-art equipment with state-of-the-art training, succumbed to human error. But none of these human errors was a straightforward mistake you can easily identify. In the first case, there was no indication that someone, say the captain, made a judgment call and opted to turn off the autopilot. In the final moments, the crew seemed to be just as surprised and confused as anyone just entering the flight deck might have been to find themselves less than two thousand feet above the ground — so surprised, in fact, that they didn't immediately react to the information. In the second case, the closest investigators could get to a root cause were garbled communications, miscommunication, and failure to identify and act on the "right" summations.

In all these cases, otherwise capable, highly trained individuals were caught in patterns of unfortunate circumstances that led to even more unfortunate decisions that led to tragic events. Human error, unintended effects, flawed assumptions, organizational lapses — these were some of the official conclusions from these and related accidents. In two of these cases, a basic question emerged: "Who was flying the plane?"

The result of all this was mandatory CRM training for pilots and flight crew members. The deficit was not in technical information or operations; it was in the stuff that happens when humans work with one another. CRM covers things like self-awareness, situational awareness, how to gather and assess crew member input, the impact of fatigue on performance and judgment, and the impact of stress and how to reduce it.

### WE ARE ALL MANAGERS, AND EVERYBODY TAKES PART

In our industry and in human services organizations generally, all these things sound familiar, don't they? Even more so when we think specifically about trauma and how to be responsive to it, as opposed to reactive. Human interaction is what we do. We don't have any complicated machines to operate or maintain — this, people working with people, is our bread and butter. Good communication, managing stress, fatigue, and burnout; resolving and sometimes avoiding unproductive conflict; managing shifting events, messed-up timetables, and unexpected changes; making judgment calls at a moment's notice with limited information — it's what we do!

Oh, wait a minute. Did you think I was talking about management and leadership? Nope. I'm talking about what happened last night just after dinner at any given waiver site or Intermediate Care Facility (ICF). The first thing we have to remember about what we do — providing services to people with disabilities — is that we are all in management. We all manage something. Some of us may manage the activities of people, but even (and especially) DSPs manage events, processes, and actions. It's what makes human services organizations unique. There are no widgets being made here. The activities usually reserved as management activities, like planning, allocating resources, decision-making, implementing those decisions, and evaluation, are all stuff DSPs do every day. When we think about what we do from this perspective, it makes sense; it feels right. What emerges is a tapestry of management activities. DSPs support the people they are with, the customer.[58] Shift leaders or site coordinators support DSPs. Managers support coordinators. Directors support managers, and so on.

All of this requires managers and leaders — who deal constantly with change anyway and are now implementing a rather large change in the organization's culture to Trauma Responsive Care

— to reexamine the manager's role. This undertaking is massive and will not only take a long time but will end up impacting every facet of the organization. In a way, this transformation starts with our own version of Crew Resource Management.

We will learn, like airline captains learn in CRM, that during this great change of implementing Trauma Responsive Care, someone has to keep flying the plane. Things will happen while you are working on this project, like an economic downturn or regulatory changes. Other big things may happen also, like, I don't know, a global pandemic. Some of these things may change your plans and your timetables, but as we have also learned, these changes in our world, and in the outside world, make moving to Trauma Responsive Care even more important.

We will learn, like all airline crew learn in CRM, that everyone has a vital role. Every single person — customer, staff, management, board member, and stakeholder — plays a crucial part in the endeavor to make everyone feel safe, connected, and in control. Managers, for example, may be the experts in crafting policies, but DSPs are experts in assessing the policies in the real world. Their involvement and input are essential.

We will also learn, again like airline crews, that while the technical stuff is important, it is not sufficient without the basics of human interaction, such as communication and empathy, and dealing with fatigue and stress. This means helping staff to manage and improve their own emotional literacy and then learn to help others with theirs.

### Two Guiding Principles of Trauma Responsive Care

So, as we start on our second question, the Who, in our larger question of "Who does what and how?," we have to be clear about what exactly our agencies do. What we do, what we *really* do, is create, in every emerging moment, supportive and caring relationships. We don't do billable services; we have relationships and we document them. To be sure, we pull predefined billable units out of that documentation, but what leaders want their staff to do is to create ongoing supportive and caring relationships with the people they are with — and leaders, in turn, support their staff. This focus on what we really do is the first guiding principle of Trauma Responsive Care.

The statement, "Leaders support their staff" — a part of any sound management practice — leads to the second principle. This principle is as close to our own Golden Rule as we get. The best way for managers to get their staff to help the people they support to feel safe, connected, and in control is for managers to help their staff to feel safe, connected, and in control. It's as simple as that: Do unto others. This is the second guiding principle of Trauma Responsive Care.

One of the most significant tasks for leadership in implementing Trauma Responsive Care is to infuse these guiding principles into the mission and into the passions and commitments that drive that mission. When you think about it, this is not new to us. Words like *supportive* and *caring* show up in mission statements much more often than, say, *efficient maximization* or *revenue enhancement.* As we discussed previously, it's a question of alignment.[59] Are we living our mission? Have we translated it throughout our organizations?

In Part Two, as we think about the various parts of the organization and then move into what each area has to do in our overall task, it's good to take a minute and reflect on these two guiding principles.

## THE LOGIC OF TRAUMA RESPONSIVE CARE

The logic behind Trauma Responsive Care is straightforward.

*If* trauma is basically characterized by feeling unsafe and out of control,

*And* the best and fastest way for a person to feel safer and more in control is through caring and supportive human connection,

*Then* the antidote to trauma is to help a person feel safe, connected, and in control.

This syllogism immediately poses the question: "How do we help someone feel safe, connected, and in control?"[60] The answer is by practicing the CALMER Skills.[61]

This, as I mentioned earlier, is the subject of Lara Palay's book, *The Way Through: Trauma Responsive Care for Intellectual and Developmental Disability Professionals.*

Trauma Responsive Care is based in every single emerging interaction, and these interactions occur throughout each day across the whole agency. Implementing Trauma Responsive Care means getting at and impacting those interactions and connections, which means impacting every interaction throughout every day, across the whole agency. Now, we can see the logic of implementing Trauma Responsive Care, and it goes something like this:

If you want your agency to be responsive to trauma, then your staff has to make sure everyone feels safe, connected, and in control all the time, and you do this by practicing the CALMER Skills, all the time, with everyone, across the whole agency, without ceasing.

A second perspective on the logic and interconnectedness of Trauma Responsive Care is apparent through the mechanism of backward mapping to connect outcomes[62] (see Figure 3.1). This map focuses on the general outcome of long-term stability, defined as decreased risk of re-traumatization and increased support. Below this outcome, you can see an array of characteristics, such as feeling safe, connected, and in control, that must be present and reinforced for that outcome to be reached. In turn, the next layer depicts practices on the part of staff, actually practicing and then mirroring the CALMER Skills for others, especially the people they support, that need to be in place to reinforce and develop the above-mentioned characteristics over time. Then we see the actions of management to support staff in their practice of the CALMER Skills.

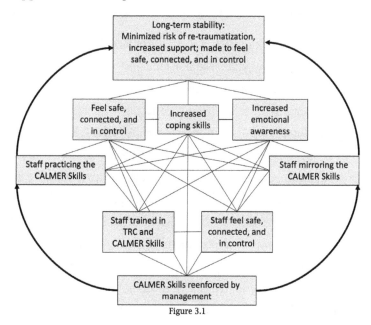

Figure 3.1

So, you see this pattern emerge:

1. The actions of management: training and supporting ...

    *Helping staff feel safe, connected, and in control.*

2. Reinforce the practices of staff: practicing and mirroring the skills for others ...

    *Helping the individual feel safe, connected, and in control.*

3. Which support the characteristics in the individual ...

*Feeling safe, connected, and in control.*

4. And support the outcome of increased stability and quality of life.

## THE THREE FOUNDATIONS OF TRAUMA RESPONSIVE CARE

All this — the guiding principles, the logic, the backward mapping, and the CALMER Skills — rests on three foundations. Trauma Responsive Care is relationally based, universally applied, and agency-wide.

### *Trauma Responsive Care Is Relationally Based*

Trauma Responsive Care requires making everyone feel safe, connected, and in control. As we've seen, the fastest road to safe and in control is through being connected with caring human beings. These safe, stable relationships are the basis for healing from trauma. The heart of Trauma Responsive Care is relationship. If we were making quality hardwood furniture, the heart of what we do would be high-quality hardwood. This comparison should make clear just how fundamental this is. Remember, what we do, what we really do, is create, in every emerging moment, supportive and caring relationships.

What does this mean? As Palay explains, Trauma Responsive Care is *our* job. It's not something we do to others — this is not a treatment or program that we administer to the people we support. Trauma Responsive Care is our own responsiveness. That's why and how Trauma Responsive Care can be implemented alongside virtually all systematic treatment approaches or milieus.

This is also why and how Trauma Responsive Care fits so well with other relational, people-first approaches like Person-Centered

Planning, Gentle Teaching,[63] positive identity, and other positive psychological approaches.[64]

### *Trauma Responsive Care Is Universally Applied*

Palay also states that Trauma Responsive Care must be applied as an emotional universal precaution, calling it an idea so brilliant it's easily missed.[65] In fact, we recommend to all agencies we work with at Aldridge Palay to couple standard first aid training, covering universal precautions in administering first aid, with refresher training in Trauma Responsive Care, because the concept of universal precaution works so well with both.

Employing the idea of universal precaution with Trauma Responsive Care is really quite simple — you apply it to everyone, regardless of what you know or don't know about that person's struggle with trauma.

Trauma Responsive Care doesn't say care that is responsive only to the trauma we know about. This gets at the question of assessment. This is how we operate, isn't it? This is how we do what we do — we assess need, we write a plan to meet that need, and we document that we've implemented the plan until the need is met or the plan changed to better meet the assessed need. So, should we assess for trauma? Yes, we should, and there are a few good available screening tools, many connected with making a Post-Traumatic Stress Disorder diagnosis. Remember, though, there are two kinds of trauma, "Big T" trauma (sexual or physical attack, war, major accident, natural disaster, and the like) and also "little t" trauma (these are events that are comparatively minor causes of pain, embarrassment, or stress — the damage comes not so much from severity as from frequency).[66]

Gathering information on "Big T" events is hard enough, but "little t"? I will repeat what Palay says about this. "I've seen many versions of screening tools that identify 'Big T's' in someone's life. I've never yet seen an instrument that can measure how many times in a day someone feels ignored, misunderstood, devalued, or overwhelmed."[67]

So, we assess, but we go in knowing the inherent weakness of the results. In our field of supporting people with I/DD with "Big T" traumas, we haven't gotten accurate counts yet, and with "little t," there's no way to count them at all.[68] Sometimes we simply don't know the story, especially when a person may receive services and supports in various forms their whole lives. But also, no matter what branch of human services we're working in, most of us simply can't know the story, because we don't have the right to — it's confidential information.[69]

Also, Trauma Responsive Care is not clinical care that is responsive to trauma. It is clinically informed, to be sure, through research in brain sciences and in trauma treatment, just to name a few key areas of research support.[70] But it is not just for a clinical environment, it's for all environments. Which makes it a perfect companion to in-depth and specialized trauma treatment. Those of us who are not clinicians may not be an active part of treatment, but we are a supportive part of treatment even though we often have very little clinical or treatment-related information.

At times, this may seem difficult, but these obstacles are not insurmountable. As I said above, we can still help someone to feel safe, connected, and in control. Consider this: We worked with an agency that had two divisions, outpatient mental health services and foster and treatment foster care. For the clinical staff, who worked with trauma a lot already, we provided a few new insights, as the staff was already quite well-versed in trauma and trauma treatment. What the agency sought was a way to get the other side of the organization, the foster parents and support staff, up to par and on the same page as the clinical staff. Obviously, the foster parents didn't provide the clinical services, but they were the vehicle for the clinical work to be carried out through the rest of the day and week. Trauma Responsive Care provided that training vehicle and also provided a common language. Now, for example, instead of trying to convey some level of urgency, while facing limitations in how much information could be shared, the clinician could simply say we need to put a little extra effort into helping the child feel safe, connected, and in control. The common understanding and language bridged the gap.

### Trauma Responsive Care Is Agency-Wide

When we implement Trauma Responsive Care, we must widen this perspective to a concept of universal application. This means we apply Trauma Responsive Care in every interaction, across the whole agency — not just with those we know have been exposed to trauma-inducing events in their lives, not just with those with behaviorally oriented goals on their plan, not just those we support — everyone. That's right, everyone! We have to universally apply this universal application (just keep reading — you'll get it).

When we think about the idea of Trauma Responsive Care as an emotional universal precaution — treating everyone as if they could benefit from feeling safe, connected, and in control — along with the concept of Trauma Responsive Care as organization-wide, it helps to think of these two ideas as the X and Y axes of a graph (see Figure 3.2). The horizontal axis is applying Trauma Responsive Care as an emotional universal precaution across all programs in the organization, while the vertical axis is applying Trauma Responsive Care up and down the whole organization chart. This means that treating everyone "as if" applies to everyone, not just the customers, consumers, or residents — *everyone*.

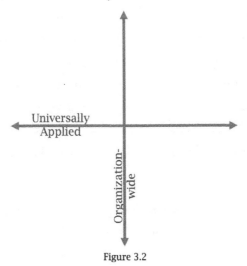

Figure 3.2

When we say we want everyone in the organization to actively try to make the person they are with at any moment feel safe, connected, and in control, we have to mean just that. Everyone must be trained, not only operations staff. Everyone's conception of the mission must be altered to include safe, connected, and in control. Everyone must be reminded to think of their job, their role, and their impact differently.

How important is this? How do you know when you've arrived? How about this: When you think that the receptionist should try to make the delivery person to feel safe, connected, and in control — better yet, when your receptionist thinks it's part of their job to help the delivery person feel safe, connected, and in control — you've got it. To accomplish this level of impact is monumental and quite difficult, but it is essential. If you are satisfied with implementing Trauma Responsive Care in only part of the organization, you leave your organization with a rather pervasive and exposed weakness.

Be mindful, however, of the sometimes gradual and incremental nature of this kind of deep change in attitude and perception, discussed in the last chapter ("Rely on Persuasion" and "Nurture Change Where It Grows"). The balance is always striving for universal application even while some parts of the organization will catch on more quickly than others. And because our organizations are always in flux, this also means, practically, that it is a continuous effort. In essence, being responsive to trauma must be at the heart of an obsession with continuous quality improvement.

These foundations are all interconnected. They must be etched into the corporate mind and maintained through rehearsal, exercise, and discussion.

I remember an old story from childhood. A man walks into a cement contractor's office and explains that he'd like to arrange for a foundation of concrete to be laid. The contractor pulls out some paperwork and says, "We can do that. How long do you want it?"

"Well," our guy says, a bit confused, "I'm going to need it forever. I'm going to build my house on it."

Together, these elements make up the foundation on which you will build. You'll want to keep them forever.

## What Does This Mean for Leadership?
As we move into Part Two of this book and look in more depth at the three-part question, "Who does what and how?" and see who

in the organization does what, we should remember that in a sense, the overall task of actually implementing Trauma Responsive Care belongs to leadership. The job of actually taking on the responsibility, making the decisions, allocating the resources, and evaluating the progress of implementing Trauma Responsive Care falls on leadership. That enormous task starts and ends with these guiding principles and these foundations.

As noted in the introduction, this book is a guide, a map, if you will, to implementing Trauma Responsive Care (Part Three). And so, it is constructed with references back and forth in the process, allowing for a bit more conceptual angle if you need it, while providing a step-by-step angle as well. So, if things stall, there are plenty of ways to regain some control and get things rolling again.

And in this larger sense, when you think about your organization's history, culture, and mission, when you contemplate meaning, if in those moments you feel disconnected or unsure, make your way back to these guiding principles and these foundations and things will look clearer.

part two
.....................................................................................................................

# Who Does What and How?

"Heaven ne'er helps the one who will not act."

—Sophocles

## chapter four

## *Who* Does What and How? The Three Components of the Organization

> "Management is doing things right,
> leadership is doing the right things."
>
> —Peter Drucker

I'm a big fan of servant leadership,[71] all the way through to the inverted organizational chart that moves top management off the top line and puts them at the bottom, supporting a hierarchy that now puts the people in the organization who work directly with the customers at the top of the chart. This concept of servant leadership is widely known in the business world and is very popular among mission-driven organizations, regardless of their tax-filing status. And, quite frankly, it should be — it's a good thing. In fact, it is at the heart of this book.

When I had the privilege to oversee policy at the Ohio Department of Developmental Disabilities, I told my staff — in areas like early childhood education, dual diagnosis (I/DD and mental illness), and autism — that they were the content experts and so they told me what needed to be done, not the other way around. My job, and my boss's job, was to listen and turn their insights into policy as much as we could, given the myriad different influences, priorities, and external considerations along the way.

But this approach to leadership from the perspective of servanthood and support must also navigate the manager's paradox, discussed in Chapter Two, and beautifully summed up in the words of Peter Drucker at the opening of this chapter. Managers must manage current systems, to "minimize risk and to keep the current system operating." And they must create and build and transition to new systems, "which in turn demands leadership."[72]

So, as we talk about who does what and how in this second part, we first have to understand that managers have a dual role. They have to manage, or make sure everyone has the time, resources, and direction to do their part; and they have to lead, forge a new way of doing what the organization does, and be, at the same time, truly responsive to trauma, to make sure everyone feels safe, connected, and in control.

But, alas, I promised in the introduction that I would stay clear of things theoretical, as I am wont to do, so that's enough of that. Let's think function!

### LEADERSHIP AND POWER

If you're a boss at any level, you will be familiar with this basic equation, even if you've never seen it expressed quite this way:

$$responsibility + authority = power$$

When you have responsibility, you should also have authority; together they generate an equal amount of power. Let's look at the first phrase, to the left of the equal sign. In a solid, well-functioning organization, this equation should be, by and large, true. If I have some responsibility over quality, then I ought to have some authority to impact quality, by measuring it or making changes to improve it and so forth. That makes sense. I don't want to be responsible for things I cannot at least partially impact.[73] This authority, added to my responsibility, gives me power, i.e., I can tell you to stop measuring this quality indicator and start measuring that indicator.

What sometimes gets away from us is what happens on the right side of the equal sign. We end up focusing on the power management and leadership have. Power to hire or discipline or fire, power to change things. Power to make things comfortable or to make things not so comfortable. We forget that the resulting power is tied to the other side of the equation. In a healthy organization, power is directly connected with responsibility and authority. In other words, power has a functional focus on making the mission happen. This functional focus on the mission and values of the organization of all elements of power in everything from operations to decision-making to strategic direction is the alignment we discussed in Chapter Three.[74]

### COMMUNICATION

For us and for our purposes of creating change in our organizations to an environment and a culture more responsive to trauma, this shifts our view of management and leadership from a construct of power to a construct of function.

In Trauma Responsive Care, every part of the organization has a role no other part can play, and every part of the organization cannot play their part without the other parts' help.

This, of course, makes communication vital. But then again, it is always vital. I once worked as an interagency planner. We helped multiple agencies supporting the same family develop and fund a wraparound plan. As planning ended, we stressed the importance of regular meetings and of keeping in close contact with the family and the other agencies involved between meetings — never stop talking. Talk, we preached — even if you think you have no reason to talk, do it anyway. Checking in when things are going well is what keeps them going well. Inevitably, on occasion we were called back in because things had fallen apart and inevitably, we would hear that the team had stopped communicating because things were going so well, they thought there was no need. Communication is the circulatory system of any enterprise and every organization. And communication lives in the central overlapping area of our Venn diagram (see Figure 4.1).

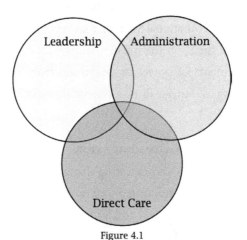

Figure 4.1

Communication cannot be taken for granted, or it will play tricks on you. I once worked with Motorola, Inc., a large American telecommunications and electronics company in Asia. Communication was their business. When I arrived in-country, I came with a small shipment of the latest cutting-edge technology to be programmed and handed out to key customers, months before it would be available to anyone else — so these customers could look cool while communicating. When I arrived at the office, I was issued a phone with all key management staff of the division entered into the directory. And it was all set up for international calls so I could communicate with my family, and they could communicate with me. Communication was their business.

The problem was that because of conflicts and innuendo and bad feelings between the various parts of the division (sales, engineering, legal, and logistics) people sitting literally five feet from each other were communicating almost exclusively through email, with ne'er a spoken word between them. They didn't fail to communicate, they just built barriers to good communication. Of course, when I dug a little deeper, I found plenty of causes for these symptoms. As one manager put it, they had forgone the benefits of direct communication to avoid any potential conflict. The cost for this false efficiency was true connection.

Throughout this book, as we talk about roles and teams and meetings and tasks in this great enterprise, and as we think more and more about helping people feel safe, connected, and in control, remember: Direct and open communication, while it may at times be messy and seem to take longer, ultimately keeps things going.

## WHO?

Now that we have the conceptual stuff taken care of, let's get down to it. As we've seen, our organizations have three major parts. These are the executive leadership, the administrative functions, and the part that does the work (see Figure 4.1). On paper, things look a lot cleaner than they are, but as we see on the Venn diagram, all these areas overlap.

In our industry, we have made good use of hybrid positions. These are positions that blend functions. For example, I've worked with agencies that have used what they called site coordinators. These positions split their time between direct care and a collection of administrative functions. So, if we were talking about management theory (which we are not!) we'd see some tasks like scheduling, specific training tasks, management of supplies, crisis support, and supervision — management tasks — performed while also performing direct service (on the clock, as it were). We would also see, in this case, that other personnel management issues, such as hiring, managing time off, and disciplinary actions were tasked to the site manager. Other blending may look like managers who also do training.

The opposite can occur as well — like managers who are freed from the tasks of hiring or disciplinary action. Or a divided management between the clinical side (managing the service plans) and the business side (managing the financial health of the site).

The point is that organizations that provide services for people with I/DD are widely varied in the details of their structures. Many different factors lend support to this or that approach, such as size, services, geographic spread, and age range of customers. We are also influenced by how we've done things in the past or by our current leadership.

Presuming that how you do things at your organization works well for you and reflects sound management practices, you will have to translate a bit as we go through the major parts of the organization. As you read on, you may realize you have positions that fit into both executive leadership and administrative staff, or both administrative staff and direct care.

That's fine. It's important to be aware of your situation and to practice here the M of the CALMER Skills, Mindfulness. "Here it just means, 'Notice what is and isn't happening *right now*'"[75] in your organization and adjust as needed.

Of course, what we are most interested in, even when we talk about the various parts of the organization, is the overall movement of the organization to a more trauma-responsive environment. Some changes, as we have seen, impact a certain segment of the whole, and some changes impact the various parts equally. Trauma Responsive Care impacts everyone. It seeks to change everyone's attitude, it gives everyone a new common language to talk about and think about becoming more responsive to trauma, and it needs to be implemented universally. So, as we have seen, we are not really interested in the various levels of power or authority throughout the three segments of the organization. We're more interested in the function of the various parts.

So, let's look at each one in a bit more detail.

### Executive Leadership

The executive leadership is basically senior management. These are the bosses and department heads. No matter how you're organized or what titles you use, every organization has this group of senior decision-makers. There's the executive director or chief executive officer (CEO), and perhaps a person in charge of operations, what the agency does for its customers. This chief operating officer (COO) may have senior operational department heads reporting to them. There are also the heads of support systems, like human resources, or the chief people officer (CPO), as some have started to call it, and the chief financial officer (CFO).[76] This group has the power in their respective areas because they have the responsibility and the authority in those areas. They take on the larger questions of management, such as how to spend resources, whether to launch a new service or create a new position. They do all the strategic planning and then figure out how to implement and then evaluate the plan.

There are things this part of the agency has to do because no other part can, but a large part of what they do they actually *cause* to be done and rather than physically doing it themselves. This makes their function in implementing Trauma Responsive Care unique.

Let's look at an example. Let's say an organization reviews its policies and decides a few need to be updated and that the organization also needs to add a few. One way to look at this is through a lens of power, as we have seen. From this perspective, the senior management team has the power to update existing policies and write new ones because they have the responsibility and the authority. But there are a couple things to consider. First, they don't have the power to write new policy willy-nilly. Their job is ultimately to make sure the organization has policies that adequately address the current and emerging needs of the organization and its stakeholders (customers, their families, regulatory agents, etc.). Second, they can't operate in a vacuum. They may *cause* the review of policy and they may even participate in the review, but they can't do it all themselves. They have the responsibility and the authority, which gives them the power, but they don't have all the information.[77] To be done right, this process needs input from all levels, not just the bosses. They may need to consult those with certain expertise. They need input from those the policy most directly affects. And, as we have already seen, if the bosses are too involved in one or more

particular projects, one might well ask who's doing the overall function of management? Who's flying the plane?

### Administrative Staff

The administrative staff are all the important parts in the middle.
This includes frontline supervisors and all the middle management,
as well as support professionals, like psychologists and therapists. It
also includes those positions we usually think of as administrative
staff — all the back-office stuff, from trainers to payroll clerks to
maintenance technicians.

I use the word *important* here for good reason. In my experience
with many organizations across the human services spectrum and
beyond, I have found this part of the organization to be the most
connected, the most influential, and, yes, the most important part of
the organization, partly because it is so diverse. When we're talking
about getting the work of the organization done and especially
when we're talking about changing the organization, this group of
people is the linchpin. They really hold everything together.

On a whim, I once did an informal analysis of position-to-
position contacts in the agency I was running at the time — basically
I charted out what positions had the most contact with others in
the organization, looking at both sheer volume and variety. I found
that the real power brokers, if relationships have anything to do
with power, all lived in this administrative part of the organization.
In the office, it was the clerical staff and payroll and HR personnel.
In operations, it was the site coordinators. These few positions had
administrative duties, and only one, the office manager, was tech-
nically "management." When I did this, a whole range of observa-
tions and gut feelings started to make more sense. If management

was implementing some change and we got this crew on board, it was pretty much smooth sailing. If this group rolled their eyes, we were sunk.

In *The Way Through*, Palay talks about how we think we (our brains) learn from the top down, through understanding abstract ideas (the cortex), when in fact, we learn from the bottom up. We have to feel safe (via our limbic system) before our abstract reasoning can fully function.[78] Likewise, we management types like to talk about change from the top down (senior management engagement). But really, if it's from anywhere, it's from the middle out. A rule of thumb in Trauma Responsive Care: Invest in the middle. That's where the power is.

### *Direct Care Staff: The People Who Do the Work of the Agency*
We're talking here about Direct Support Professionals and other positions that have sustained and direct contact with the final customer, the people the agency supports. Right now, though, as we think about the *who* in the organization, it's important to think about the role as larger than the position. The whole agency is involved in organizing, supporting, and even perfecting the mission. But these people are the ones who actually *do* the mission, day in and day out.

In an earlier discussion, we saw that even though we pull predefined billable services out of the documentation (timesheets, ratio counts, unit counts, goals addressed, meds administered, etc.), what we really do is provide supportive, caring relationships through person-to-person interactions. These are the people who actually do that. We also saw that something particular to human services organizations is that we all do some sort of management.

We don't make widgets, we make relationships, and these relationships cannot be directly dictated. Supervisors are not little puppet masters pulling strings to dictate what DSPs do next. We can train, we can discuss, we can rehearse, but ultimately, Direct Support Professionals are out there doing their work, that's why we call them Direct Support *Professionals* — *they* are making decisions, *they* are making judgment calls, *they* are doing the work! And if we ask them, as we are doing, to help the people they support to feel safe, connected, and in control, we have to equip them and support them and ultimately trust them to do just that.

## THE RULE OF THREE

Now that we have laid out the *who* in our larger question of "Who does what and how?" we can move on to *what*? But first let me answer a question that may have emerged for you. This book is a guide to implementing Trauma Responsive Care and we presented, in Chapter Three, a brief description of exactly what Trauma Responsive Care is. But why, in this book about implementing Trauma Responsive Care, would we talk about who is doing the various tasks of implementing before we talk about the tasks themselves?

That's a good question. The answer is the rule of three. You probably noticed that when we talked earlier about the foundations of Trauma Responsive Care, there were three. That trend carries on. As we just discussed, the structures of our organizations tend to fall into three major parts. Even if we have multiple divisions, like waiver services, ICF services, and overlapping mental health services, we tend to create similar but tailored administrative bands and corresponding direct care capacity for each division. You may have two or more divisions, but the overall structure of leadership, administration, and doing the work is still the ultimate foundation.

Likewise, we will see there are three major tasks to be completed when implementing Trauma Responsive Care and three core strategies or tools used to complete these tasks. So, you can see the rule of three emerging. The rule builds on the natural correspondence of structure, resources (time and money), and people with tasks in any group activity, from a book club to a Fortune 500 multinational corporation. So, if an organization has a task that is necessary, has some cost attached to it, and is repeated with some frequency, that organization will have corresponding structure, resource allocation, and people power dedicated to that task.

Simply stated, the rule of three is this: The three major elements of a human services organization (who) each take the lead in one of the three general tasks of implementing Trauma Responsive Care (what), and each task is best completed using one of three tried-and-true strategies (how). This is a correlation, not an exclusive pairing, as we shall see. And the correlation has also to do with the time it takes to complete each of the three tasks of implementing Trauma Responsive Care. Before we continue with the other parts of our question, the what and the how, we must lay the groundwork of the rule of three. We will do this based on what we have already covered — the who — so the other questions will fall neatly into place.

It's best to think of this rule through a combined diagram. We've already used the Venn diagram to show the three parts of our organizations (the who) and overlapping nature of these three component parts. That provides an important perspective, and we'll revisit it as we go. Now, we'll think of the parts using the metaphor of swim lanes, as seen in Figure 4.2.

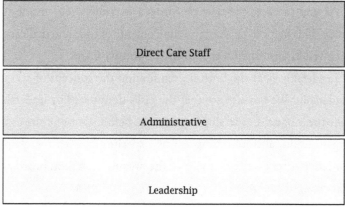

Figure 4.2

You can see the three parts of the organization with leadership and senior management on the bottom, the administrative sector in the middle and the direct care staff on the top. As we build on this diagram, it will help us place the other questions of what and how in relation to the who.

Now let's add a triangle. (Figure 4.3)

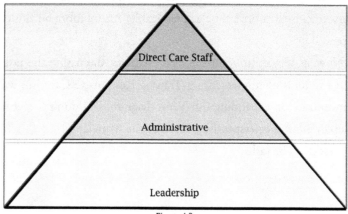

Figure 4.3

As you can see, the triangle forms a pyramid shape inside our lanes. This helps us understand the elements of time and dedication involved in implementing Trauma Responsive Care.

Leadership is at the bottom, reinforcing the concept of servant leadership. We can also see that the tasks dominated by leadership take the longest. Leadership begins work before everyone else in the organization, and leadership is busy, specifically with the change initiative, after every other part of the organization is on board and has changed course.

The administrative band, the linchpin of the whole thing, is in the middle, sitting on the firm foundation of dedicated leadership and supporting the top, or the point of the organization, the Direct Support Professionals. I hope you caught the pun because it was intended. The point of our pyramid is the whole point of the organization.

In terms of time, the pyramid within our lanes also reinforces the fact, as we shall discuss later, that for the most impact, we will want to concentrate training so that we reach critical mass of trained personnel in as short a time as practicable. Again, more on timing later.

Now, as we continue in the next chapters, discussing the tasks and the tools of implementing Trauma Responsive Care, we will concentrate on expanding our Venn diagram. But don't forget to keep in mind the perspective offered by the swim lanes.

First up: The tasks.

## chapter five

## Who Does *What* and How? The Three Tasks of Implementing Trauma Responsive Care

"Build to-day, then, strong and sure,
    With a firm and ample base;
    And ascending and secure
    Shall to-morrow find its place."
                    —Henry Wadsworth Longfellow[79]

You may remember the story I told of the two bricklayers in Chapter Two, when we were discussing the need to create a vision. The story makes its point for creating a vision — you have to keep everyone's eyes on the prize. Now we can think with a bit more generosity about the other guy, the first bricklayer. The truth is you need both perspectives — the wider and inspiring vision and a keen focus on the task at hand. And leadership has to manage both.

Since this change to be responsive to trauma is a change in your corporate culture, and is both highly intensive and wide in scope, it must, like every complex situation, be broken into manageable parts — and these parts into even smaller, more manageable parts. So, as we go through the tasks of implementing Trauma Responsive Care, we are going to view them by relating the general tasks with the specific. Training is a good example. We will discuss training under the general task of equipping staff. It is easy in the everyday rush of life to think of training staff as a particular job to be done, like another brick in the wall. And we may have things in place to make sure we do this particular task with a high level of quality. But we also have to make sure we complement our laser focus on the particular with the larger picture — we are not only teaching staff to do particular things in particular ways. We are increasing understanding and insight as well. Through this training, we are equipping staff to live out the mission.

## THE THREE TASKS OF IMPLEMENTING TRAUMA RESPONSIVE CARE

Now let's think about the second *W* question: What? What are the things we have to do to create this change?

There are, on an organizational level, three major tasks in implementing Trauma Responsive Care. They are equipping the organization with Trauma Responsive Care, managing organizational investment in Trauma Responsive Care, and building the sustainability of Trauma Responsive Care.

### *Equipping the Organization*

The most concrete and active part of implementing Trauma Responsive Care or any trauma responsive systemic approach is the training. Eventually, everyone has to be trained.

As we discussed above, a truly trauma responsive environment is not an "approach" or an "intervention." In order for this responsiveness to work and really sink into the nature of how the organization thinks and feels about itself — what it is and what it does — everyone must strive to help everyone else feel safe, connected, and in control. So, senior managers and the CEO can't say, "My staff need to know this, but I don't have time to go through this training." The accounts receivable clerk and the HR manager can't think, "I have little direct contact with our consumers, so I don't have to worry about this." Everyone must be trained.

Now, if you think about this and do your own math, you might think given a large number of staff, and only so much time — this could take a while. It could, though every organization is different.

While you're thinking about training current staff, remember you have turnover (like you could forget!). So, you also have to ensure there is training in place for new staff coming on board. This means augmenting your training for new staff. Then, like all training of this sort, you have to devise a way to build refresher training into your annual or biennial training practices.

Training is an enormous task, and it is a large project to manage just by itself. It could take, depending on the organization, up to a year to thoroughly complete the training. In the next part, we will look at some concrete strategies to help make this project within a project easier to manage. For now, though, remember you can jump-start this process by training a critical mass of roughly 60% of your staff in the initial drive.[80] Just like in advertising, it's best to saturate your staff in the initial stages through the training drive and through other means (see the discussion on building sustainability below).

For now, though, I must stress that the training is not the whole initiative. If it is not strengthened by changes in the formal, long-term life of the organization through policies, procedures, tools, and the like (organizational investment), and if it is not reinforced in the thoughts and feelings of the organization through various flows of information and discussion (building sustainability), then it will disappear as quickly as it is implemented.

## Organizational Investment

This task encompasses investing the values and practices of Trauma Responsive Care into the everyday procedural life of the organization. And I use the word *investing* exactly how you probably read it — putting effort and resources in now in order to realize a future gain, to get a return. This is the long game, and the task here is to impact strategic direction for the next five, ten, or twenty years of operations.[81]

It's helpful to think of this as the hard side of the organization and it is made up of stuff you can touch — literally, you can pick it up and hand it to someone. Think of the tangible, written side of the organization's life. This includes all the nuts and bolts of daily operations, like forms and training materials, but also the visionary expressions, like mission and value statements, not to mention all policies and procedures.[82]

Reflecting Trauma Responsive Care in the written, formal aspects of the organization ensures the values and commitments of Trauma Responsive Care have a good chance of living beyond the tenure of current leadership or champion. And this task includes a systematic review of the entire written life of the organization. In Chapter Two, we discussed this task as the need to institutionalize the change.

The best approach to this is through a trauma-informed or trauma-responsive organizational assessment. If done right, a solid assessment will allow you to immediately grasp the obvious, like changes in training procedures to account for refresher training in Trauma Responsive Care. It will also help identify more subtle aspects of change, like manager trainings and discussions that create and then reinforce a new management style. Overall, there are four key areas you need to assess, though in Part Three, I provide a more detailed list.

- Policies and procedures (including mission and vision statements)
- Practices for hiring, training, and supporting staff
- Management style
- Collaborative practices

There are obvious elements of interaction and interdependence in these areas, so as you thoroughly assess one, you will gain insights into the others as well. However you opt to complete the assessment, it will build on itself and, as the work continues, create its own momentum toward change. Although it will seem at first like an insurmountable task, eventually, the tool or mechanism you use will become something that helps organize and lead the process. The tool itself becomes a written record, part of the long-term trajectory of the organization. It becomes a mechanism for identifying and changing policies, procedures, and practices in an orderly way that improves sustainability and avoids chaos.

As your organization does its annual planning, a discussion of Trauma Responsive Care should be a part of it, reflected in training and events planning and in resource allocation. It should also become a central tenet of longer-term strategic planning.

You can think of this as the overall course for an ocean liner sailing across the sea — some corrections and adjustments are made along the way, but the overall task is to stay the course. But what about the beginning of the journey — leaving the dock and navigating the harbor?

### *Building Sustainability*

The third task of implementing Trauma Responsive Care is building sustainability, and it is best seen as related to organizational investment. Building sustainability impacts the soft side of the organization and is made up of the stuff you can feel. This is where corporate culture lives and it reflects the many connections between our various perceptions, attitudes, and values — it is how the organization thinks and feels about itself and how it confronts challenges and makes decisions. This intangible soul of the organization is where the power of sustainability comes from. In terms of implementing Trauma Responsive Care, it is the short game to organizational investment's long game. And where organizational investment was concerned mostly with the last two lessons[83] on change in Chapter Two, building sustainability is concerned with just about all the other lessons.[84]

#### THE FOUR R'S: REMEMBER, REINFORCE, REFINE, REPEAT

While the task of organizational investment contains, say, writing a formal policy and accompanying materials to train staff on trauma, the task of building sustainability contains the seriousness with which the policy is lived out. As we have seen, it involves the more rarified aspects of organizational life, such as understanding and commitment, management style and culture, and, most practically, memory — institutional memory.

Excitement and commitment must be nurtured from the top down and so, as the long task of training is rolled out, managers must form the habits of this new perspective with each other over and over again, until they are second nature: safe, connected, and in control! When managers remember, they can then reinforce these new values throughout their part of the organization. And the best way to reinforce new values is by doing routine tasks in a new way, using new tools.

In the beginning, as the initiative is introduced and the first trainings take place, all of the activities will keep the initiative in everyone's mind. Getting people throughout the organization to think in terms of helping people to feel safe, connected, and in control will be relatively easy as it is fresh and new. So, one way to think about this task, is as a big internal ad campaign — it bridges the gap between initial excitement and the deeper return on the investments of policy and structural change.

This task of building sustainability must begin to embed the values into everyday organizational life. Here, the values of Trauma Responsive Care become the *language of the job*.

And the quickest way to learn a new language is quite simple — use it! Talk about it! Hold impromptu and planned discussions about trauma, about the brain on trauma, about your own fear reactions, about what makes you feel safe, connected, and in control. Building this new language of responsiveness refines everyone's perspective and drives the change deeper into the culture.

And...

...repeat.

Building this new language of responsiveness refines everyone's perspective and drives the change deeper into the culture.

See what I did there?

The way I've described this task may feel a bit frenetic, but it will begin to feel more comfortable as you continue the process. Again, as the investment is made in the long-term strategic direction, this softer, more emotional aspect of organizational life becomes more settled and more congruent with the harder, more tangible side. At the beginning, however, you really are spending a lot of time reminding everyone of the change and keeping the vision clearly in view.[85] Sustainability, especially in the early stages must be carried in this new language. Trauma Responsive Care contains phrases and mnemonic devices, such as "safe, connected, and in control" and "CALMER" precisely to create a new language, a new standard for quality.[86]

## THE RULE OF THREE

We've covered the three tasks of implementing Trauma Responsive Care in their general form. In Part Three of this book, we will get much more detailed in exactly what to do when. For now, though, let's get back to the rule of three and see how the *who* relates to the *what*. Remember the rule of three is relatively simple: the three components of an organization, the three tasks of implementing Trauma Responsive Care, and the three strategies used in implementation all relate to each other in an overall system to create a sustainable trauma-responsive environment.

In Figure 4.1 on page 62, we used a Venn diagram to see each major part of the human services organization in relation to one another. Now we can add the tasks to this same diagram to reveal the next layer of the rule of three (see Figure 5.1).

Figure 5.1

The relationships are not exclusive but represent more of a correlation, an emphasis or concentration of effort. You may recall the example of policy development I used when discussing leadership in Chapter Four. Leadership may cause the review of policy and they may even participate in the review, but they can't do it all themselves. Keep this in mind as we review the relationship between the various parts of an organization and the tasks necessary for implementing Trauma Responsive Care.

### Leadership and Organizational Investment
Anything we might say generally about the role of senior leadership in an organization, like planning, setting strategic direction, allocating resources, evaluation, and correction for the whole organization, we can say with equal force about the role of senior leadership in implementing Trauma Responsive Care. All the things involved with the task of organizational investment — assessing, reviewing, and changing policy, along with creating a sense of urgency and

"selling" the vision — fall squarely on the shoulders of leadership. After all, the list of lessons from change management in Chapter Two, are all, at their core, aimed at senior management, either as something they must do or something they must cause to be done.

In fact, the alignment of leadership with the activities and concerns we called the task of organizational investment is so thorough, so obvious, it can easily be overlooked or oversimplified.

It is said that wins are attributable to the players while losses are on the coach. Since every decision and the responsibility to review every decision is on senior management's to-do list, in business of any kind, this sports adage is quite literally true.[87]

But we must also consider the separate aspects of *doing* a thing and *making sure a thing gets done*. In a real sense, all the tasks belong to leadership when we think about *making sure it gets done*.[88] The relationship of leadership and organizational investment focuses more on leadership's role of the actual *doing*. From our list of lessons, leadership is concerned mostly with these five:

- Communicate
- Build a sense of urgency
- Create a vision
- Institutionalize the change
- Evaluate continually

But the two that are most in force, especially in the tasks of organizational investment, are institutionalizing and continuous evaluation. Even so, given what has to be done in the remaining tasks, if you're thinking that the role of leadership is actually much broader than the activities involved in organizational investment in implementing Trauma Responsive Care, you're right. And you are beginning to see how the systems approach works.

### *Administrative Staff and Building Sustainability*

Let's start with the items on the list of lessons for change management and see which of those are associated with the task of building sustainability:

- Communicate
- Build a sense of urgency
- Create a vision
- Rely on persuasion
- Nurture change where it grows
- Grab short-term wins

Any one of these items may involve senior management to varying degrees and not just administrative staff and frontline supervisors. But when you think about the actions involved, say, with the four R's or relaying and discussing the vision, you can see that the bulk of this work involves the middle, administrative band, especially frontline supervisors. A boss may craft the vision, but giving it life and meaning for everyone, including the part-time third-shifter, is on the frontline supervisor.

### *Direct Care and Equipping Staff*

The relationship of direct care and the task of equipping staff is the most straightforward and is mostly a task of participation. The actions of equipping — developing training, training, reinforcing training — are actions most likely done by the administrative sphere, but the impact, which is what we are most concerned with, is with everyone in the organization, especially operational staff. It's in our first guiding principle: What we do, what we *really* do, is create, in every emerging moment, supportive and caring relationships. Equipping and supporting staff to do this encompasses the whole organization.

## BRINGING IT TOGETHER: WORD AND DEED

In all of this, along with an element of action, there is an element of participation. There is, for example, teaching the CALMER Skills, and there is implementing them (reminding, reviewing, and refining the use of the CALMER Skills). So, each role, and each task associated with that role, are all connected and interdependent.

Let's take a deeper look at an example I used earlier — creating a vision. Senior management must create a sense of urgency and must then create the vision of a new future. This sense of urgency and the vision must then be communicated and supported. This involves talking with and persuading department heads, managers, support personnel, and supervisors. They in turn carry the message of the new vision through the ranks of the whole organization.

This new vision honed and given legitimacy through top leadership is played out in word and deed. The words — talking about it, persuading others, discussing it to develop a deeper understanding — are all part of building sustainability, and middle management (administration) does this work. The deeds — revamping the mission statement, expressing the vision in formal communications, updating policy to operationalize the vision, solidifying the vision as the agenda of the board — are all part of organizational investment, and the bosses do this work. Directing both word and deed to everyone in the organization, especially Direct Support Professionals, is the beginning of equipping staff.

Now, to complement this affiliation between the general tasks to be done and the part of the organization most fully involved with each, we can add three strategies that are widely used to get things done in businesses of all kinds in the next chapter. These strategies, in turn, reveal their own natural connection to who does what in implementing Trauma Responsive Care.

## chapter six

## Who Does What and *How*? The Three Strategies to Make It Happen and Make It Stick

"The best way to predict the future is to create it."

—Peter Drucker

Business is constantly looking for better ways to get things done. The things that really work have become second nature to us — so ubiquitous we sometimes don't even notice them — like the way our organizations are structured. The service- or region-based[89] divisional organizational structure is found in virtually every human services organization everywhere (or any kind of organization, for that matter). It came from the desire, or need, for the modern organization to do more than one thing at the same time. When Henry Ford dominated the car market because he had solved the problem of production, he failed to see the emerging problem of marketing. He famously quipped, "They can have any color they want, as long as it's black." Alfred Sloan at General Motors didn't miss the next competitive wave. He developed the product-based divisional management structure. By innovating the organizational structure, as Henry Ford had done with manufacturing (the assembly line), Sloan changed the competitive game. It seems so basic to us now, but this relatively young innovation in organizational life suddenly allowed one organization to do multiple complex things (like waiver services, mental health services, and an ICF or two) at the same time with amazing efficiency.[90]

While this service- or region-based divisional structure adds efficiency, it also adds complexity. So, in this chapter concentrating on the question of how we will accomplish the tasks of implementing Trauma Responsive Care, it's a good place to start.

When an agency has more than one division, related but distinct, it may have more than one culture. There may be an overarching style or feel that emerges from the mix of perceptions, attitudes, and values in one division or location that is different in another — even though both are fed from the same stream of mission and value statements and the same overall leadership. And so, the behaviors, operational habits, and decision-making within each division may differ. This is not necessarily a bad thing, but it is a thing. In fact, if you could trace particular values — say, valuing safety for the people supported along with a commitment to their dignity in taking risks — throughout a large agency, you are bound to find variations on how these values are balanced, with some divisions or subdivisions or locations emphasizing this or that side of the equation.

This reality echoes back to our discussion of the lessons on managing change in Chapter Two, specifically that we must rely on persuasion and that we must nurture change where it grows.

Within the bounds of how we structure our organizations, we can deduce that the best strategies or approaches to getting something done are the strategies we already know and use regularly, even though we may not think of them as strategies for implementing change. We're going to use three tried-and-true strategies you are already familiar with to implement Trauma Responsive Care. Their power is amplified in connecting these three ways to get things done with the tasks we need to get done and the parts of the organization that will do them.

Our structural orientation also means that as we discuss the three strategies on which we will rely, we have to remember that each of our divisions or subdivisions is a living, breathing thing, so within our three strategies, our particular approaches may differ.

### The Three Strategies for Implementing Trauma Responsive Care

A few months before we got married, my bride-to-be and I took a bus from Ottawa, Illinois, two hours downstate to Rantoul to pick up our first car from my father. It was a 1978 AMC Gremlin.[91] When we got there, my dad gave me a small toolbox containing a hammer, a couple of wrenches, and a few basic screwdrivers, along with a few other specifically automotive tools. He popped open the little hatchback and placed the toolbox in the car. "This will get you started," he said to me, "and you're gonna need 'em."

The three strategies for implementing Trauma Responsive Care are well-known to us and we already use them quite a bit. They are the use of teams, the use of tools, and project management. Like the hammer, wrenches, and screwdrivers my dad gave me, they're not sexy, but they are versatile and very powerful. And you're gonna need 'em.

### Teams

First of all, for us in this endeavor, teams are not task forces and are not committees. Task forces are for the big picture, the long view (insert your own cliché here _____). And a committee is for ... I don't really know what a committee is for. But a team is a group of people who come together to do something that any one of them cannot do as well by themselves.

A team may perform an ongoing task. For example, a team of case managers who, while maintaining their own caseloads, are interconnected and back each other up to the point of being almost interchangeable. Or a team might come together to complete a given task and then they're done. Provided they are formed and managed well, teams are amazing at concentrating expertise and commitment very efficiently.

When I worked for Motorola's Southeast Asia Cellular Infrastructure Division, my job was to get the various disciplines involved in any particular project to work together better. The two main players were sales and engineering, with sales doing all or most of the customer contact. But each proposal promised a fully cooked cellular system, complete with site development, antenna systems, switching gear, and the software that told all the little electrons what to do when. So the salesperson would inevitably end up working with manufacturing, shipping, software engineering, and legal. This team, with permeable edges and representing a multitude of factors, was complicated by cultural influences. The customer might be in Sri Lanka, sales and hardware engineering in Indonesia, manufacturing in Scotland, and the people dealing with endless details of import/export, tariffs, restrictions, taxes, etc., sat in Singapore, Hong Kong, and the United States.

Our solution was to create a vision of a focused team approach, using the crisis management scenes from *Apollo 13,* a well-known movie at that time, as a common language and metaphor for the kind of projects the division handled. Actor Ed Harris, playing the part of Gene Kranz, flight director, moves slowly on the screen, relays a few general instructions, and says, "Let's work the problem, people. Let's not make it worse by guessing." So, for two days of exercises, discussions, and role-playing, we talked about moving past all the minutiae, all the blaming and defending, all the ego, to step up with the expertise you bring to the table and "work the problem, people."

A year or so later, I was meeting with the division head who had just returned from Indonesia. He told me he approached a team to get an update on a rather tense project. "I was told," he said, "to be quiet. 'We're working the problem.'" The senior manager had lost a little control in this situation, but the team, with the expertise, had picked it up, and that was really the point.

At Motorola, these teams developed organically around a project. This is similar to how large IT and management consulting firms work. A central contact person, like an engagement director (ED) or engagement manager (EM) works with the client firm to develop the scope of work and then recruits an internal team of experts needed to implement the scope of work. You can see in this example that it would be impossible for one employee at Motorola, or an IT or consulting firm, to do all the work by themselves. Through teams, the responsibility, authority, and subsequent power transfers temporarily to the team, and things get done more thoroughly and more efficiently.

Teams are not for everything, in spite of what some think.[92] For some work, including some distinct parts of a larger project, it's better done by one person — to avoid the proverbial camel (a horse designed by committee). So, we want to use teams where the problem can better be solved by people coming together because any one of them alone cannot do it as well.

For our purposes of implementing Trauma Responsive Care, using teams is both necessary and straightforward, especially given the step-by-step guide of Part Three. Here are a few fundamental characteristics of high-performing teams:

*Clear: Set Clear and Straightforward Goals*
The team should be clear about their task and given a concise charge. The task should be specific and expressed in everyday language. Technical language is fine, but understanding the task in plain language, especially if there are multiple disciplines involved, will help the team understand the larger context. Also, if the task is expressed as a goal, the team will always have a clear understanding of when they have completed their job.

*Responsible: Give the Team the Responsibility and Authority to Act, Then Hold It Accountable*
The team must have the authority to act within its scope. Only then can it be responsible for the task and held accountable for its work. Remember the leadership/power equation in Chapter Four? It works the same with teams. When you give a team responsibility, you must also afford it authority, and together they generate an equal amount of power within the organization to do their work. Nothing will communicate a lack of leadership interest in a project more quickly than parking it with a team that has no clear responsibility or authority to act.

*Equipped: Give the Team Everything It Needs to Do the Work*
The team must be given the resources to complete the job, including a budget if the task calls for it. If the task was clear to begin with, this is not as difficult as it may first seem. Let's say you gather a team of managers with the charge of "Get comprehensive time management

training for all managers." This team had better have contract development authority and a budget so they can truly represent the organization with potential vendors. If the team, for larger budgetary
reasons, cannot be equipped with this authority and these resources,
then you have given them the wrong task. Perhaps the task is "Find
good time management training for managers, identify vendors,
and get proposals from the top three." With this charge, a team can
talk to vendors with authority, ask questions, make decisions, and
complete the task with three proposals. This task done, the finance
office may be more comfortable and can recharge the team with the
original task, along with the requisite authority and budget.

## Agile: Keep the Team Small and Responsive
The teams should be small and agile. Four to eight people is a basic
rule of thumb. Any smaller and the task is probably done better by
an individual gathering input. Any larger gets too unwieldy and will
more easily become mired or lost. A team of four to eight people can
expand and contract as needed (given they have a clear charge and
the proper authority to do so) to get the task done with a high level
of quality in a timely manner.

## Trusted: Trust the Team to Do the Work
The team has to be trusted to do its task. If you have followed
the guidelines up to this point, there is little concern here. If you
haven't, stop now. If a team is not trusted, they will figure that out
— even before you do. They will know that what they are doing
really doesn't matter and so they will not be invested. Staff will
also know that anytime management asks them to be involved in
something like this in the future, it isn't really serious, and potential team members will not be invested in that either. The story of

senior management asking people to do something when they are not truly trusted to do it is the story of the senior manager who cried wolf. Nothing you say will be taken seriously, and nothing you advocate will be taken to heart.

*Engaged: Expect the Team to Repay Your Trust through Engagement*
To succeed, team members must be engaged. It should not only be clear to them what the team is to do, it should also be clear to them why they are on the team to begin with. Again, like the last few items on this progressive list, if you have followed each step, these last few will take care of themselves. If you haven't, these last few will be nearly impossible to accomplish.

## TOOLS

The word *tool* is a complicated word. There are numerous definitions for the word as a noun, and it can also be used as a verb. There are also slang usages. You can use the word tool in a number of ways to get your meaning across. The word *tool* is, in fact, a tool. The definition we will use is the third in Webster's: "Something used in doing a job, a means to an end."[93] Dictionary.com's fifth definition is "anything used as a means to accomplish a task or purpose."[94] This is admittedly pretty broad, so I will narrow it down. But these definitions should serve to remind you to be creative in inventing your own tools to help implement Trauma Responsive Care.

First, consider this. The adjective *creative* is from the verb *to create*, which means "to cause to come into being, to make by investing, to cause to happen."[95] Did you notice that the six characteristics of high-performing teams above form the acronym CREATE?

So, when I recommend that you CREATE high-performing teams to implement Trauma Responsive Care, the recommendation itself contains the characteristics and values — the very definition — of high-performing teams. We've created a thread that associates the idea of getting things done with creating or "causing to happen." The way we have used this acronym is a mnemonic, a device or tool used to assist in remembering something.[96]

Here's another: The act of boiling the antidote to trauma down to "safe, connected, and in control" is shorthand for all of Trauma Responsive Care. By themselves, these words are little more than a sentence fragment. But as you go through Trauma Responsive Care or read *The Way Through,*[97] this fragment takes on a life of its own. It carries a larger message. It tucks facts and insights and feelings of empathy and healing under its wings and carries them. Soon, you won't remember the facts and figures or the details of this or that part of the brain. But you will remember the message. And you will remember that it carries direction and value and mission. How can I help you feel safe, connected, and in control?

The phrase "safe, connected, and in control" is a meme. A meme is a unit of cultural transmission, or a unit of imitation. It is what philosopher Daniel Dennett calls a replicator of ideas, very much like a gene replicates in biology.[98] In fact, zoologist Richard Dawkins coined the word *meme* from the longer Greek root *mimeme*, meaning imitation, to associate it, by sound, with the word *gene*, a container of genetic information for replication.[99] And, yes, this includes that picture of a cat with his face crammed into a glass of scotch, lapping it up, with the caption "Tough day" you posted on Facebook last night. It also includes that poster that every office has of the crew team rowing down the river as mist rises in the early-morning air, just above the word *TEAMWORK*. They all convey ideas that are enhanced through replication.

Mnemonics and memes are just two general tools you can use to infuse Trauma Responsive Care into the culture of your organizations. Other tools are more specific. In our work with client agencies, we use forms that help support professionals and DSPs figure out how to help someone feel safe, connected, and in control. We also have a tool, based in brain science, that guides a team through defusing a crisis. These forms help in a process, but they also serve to convey the meaning and values of Trauma Responsive Care.

As you think about the tasks of implementing Trauma Responsive Care, especially the task of building sustainability, many other tools to help you with this process will come to mind. Here are a few things clients have done, plus some space for your own ideas.

- Posters on the wall: "safe, connected, and in control" or the CALMER Skills
- Agenda items for team meetings — examples of using the Skills
- Gathering, recording, and repeating success stories in your newsletter
- Making business cards of the CALMER Skills
- Trauma Responsive Care T-shirts, given when training is completed
- Discussion or reading groups
- _____
- _____
- _____
- _____

## PROJECT MANAGEMENT

With clients, I have sometimes used the term *project manager with passion* or *internal champion*. Although it has devolved into a sales strategy,[100] originally the term *internal champion* emerged as the person in the organization, usually in upper management, who was particularly fond of a fledgling idea or product. This person had "drunk the Kool-Aid," so to speak, and was ready to use their influence and power to nurture the project and protect it from internal politics, as well as to steer investment and the allocation of resources toward it.

One of our clients came to us by way of what we would call an internal champion. The quality manager of one agency had become increasingly convinced that the agency needed to take trauma and trauma-informed care more seriously. She worked endlessly to gather information and obtain training. Her reports to senior management were more and more laced by her perception that a more robust approach to trauma was very much needed. She became like the preacher I referred to above: "You'll get the second sermon when you do something about the first."

She finally came across a recording of a webinar we did in conjunction with two national advocacy organizations on what leaders need to know about trauma and showed it to her CEO.[101] From there she contacted us, and we developed a proposal. She was relentless in pursuing what she saw was absolutely necessary for her agency if her agency was going to truly live its own mission. And she worked tirelessly to convince her bosses. Once we came into the picture, she ran the entire initiative with equal vigor.

This is a project manager with passion.

Much of this process, involving all the tasks and the entire organization, requires the overall coordination that the techniques of project management entail. We are used to, for example, the idea of tapping one highly competent manager to take an agency through its first accreditation or through a big recertification process. There are a lot of processes, a lot of people, and a lot of time involved, and a solid project manager, who buys into it all, who really believes, keeps the whole thing on track.

### BACK TO THE RULE OF THREE

Now that we have covered all three elements of all three areas contained in the Trauma Responsive Care rule of three, it will become clearer as we add the strategies to the tasks and the parts of the organization most involved in completing that task. Let's start by going back to our augmented Venn diagram (See Figure 6.1)

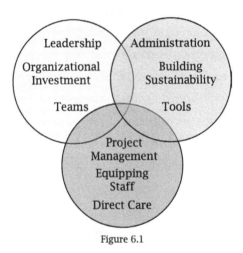

Figure 6.1

### *Leadership — Organizational Investment — Teams*

We've seen a few things line up from the start. At the beginning, we were reminded that executive leadership is ultimately responsible for the relative success or failure of the organization, and they are responsible for driving the lessons for managing big change. We also learned that while leadership is responsible for making sure every-thing gets done throughout the organization, they are also directly responsible for actually doing a few of those things. One of those things, directly from our lessons, is institutionalizing the change.

Here are a few of the important institutionalizing activities in Trauma Responsive Care:

- Assessing the entire organization regarding its familiarity with trauma and trauma-informed care, and regarding its readiness for change
- Reviewing and refining the organizational mission and vision statements
- Reviewing all policies and procedures to increase alignment with Trauma Responsive Care
- Reviewing management practices and styles to increase align-ment with Trauma Responsive Care
- Reviewing training strategies and materials to increase align-ment with Trauma Responsive Care

You will find a more comprehensive discussion in Part Three, but for now you can pick anything from this list and see how actually doing it requires input. Any one of these tasks fits perfectly into our litmus test for using teams: A group of people can do it better than any one of them can do it by themselves. To be sure, a single manager may take charge of getting these tasks done (project management), but the best way for that manager to proceed is by gathering quali-fied staff to help do it.

### *Administrative Band — Building Sustainability — Tools*
Let's think back to our discussion of the four R's in Chapter Five. They are: remember, reinforce, refine, and repeat. These tasks

of building sustainability include both the kickoff event and the smaller activities and action to keep the excitement and commitment going.

The first time I decided to go vegetarian, as a young man, I made sure I told everyone in my family and at work. I took care to announce this decision in just the right mixture of somber tones so my moral superiority was clear while my magnanimous nature shone through. I was thoughtful and I planned ahead, aware of my nemesis, the basic cheeseburger, and ready to deal with cravings through avoidance and sheer determination. After all, it was a higher calling.

The first week went great. That weekend went great. It was Tuesday before I suddenly realized that I had absentmindedly munched on some cold fried chicken while making a salad on Saturday. My problem was not the cravings. My problem was simply remembering that I was now a vegetarian. I had to put a sign up on the fridge: *Remember: You are a vegetarian now.*

The success and efficiency of our organizations — both very good things — depend on each of us diligently performing our role within the larger organization. Our heads are down and we're moving forward. For change to begin to take hold, we have to look up. Real change, especially change that goes deep into our preconscious thoughts, attitudes, and perceptions, needs first to break into our habits and preferences. Real change must cause us to examine these habits and preferences and persuade us of a different way, a better way. This takes time and discussion and consideration. Even then, we have to remember and reinforce the change. Through this process, we can refine the message and its practice.

To do this, we need to apply the strength of the middle, the administrative band, including frontline supervisors, and use every tool at our disposal. To be sure, that same project manager who called for leadership to charge teams with specific tasks in organizational investment may also spur these actions. And a team to coordinate it all might be just what the doctor ordered. But it is this team's creation and use of tools — forms, agenda items, discussions, events, contests, T-shirts, memes, mnemonics, gimmicks — that will make the difference.

### *Direct Care — Equipping Staff — Project Management*
We have already discussed the three components of training for a large-scale change like Trauma Responsive Care — training current staff, building training into new staff onboarding, and refresher training. Making sure all these get done is quintessentially a task for project management. It contains event planning and tracking, as well as building systems, including some that are time-limited and some that are ongoing. And although there are definitely parts of this task of equipping staff where having too many people involved will serve mostly to confuse things, there are plenty of uses for teams and tools as well.

In the previous chapter, I stressed that the connection between each of these groups of three is loose and more a matter of emphasis than exclusivity. This is because in all three categories — the who, the what, and the how — there is a significant amount of blending. This blending is nowhere more evident than it is here. First of all, the *who* in the task of equipping staff is everyone in the organization, even though we are primarily focused on operations staff — the people who do the work of the organization. This broad stroke is also clear in the task itself. Equipping staff is, again, mostly concerned with getting everyone trained in Trauma Responsive Care. But it doesn't stop there. The work involved with building sustainability interacts with equipping staff as a melding of training and teaching in order to produce insight and change.

When I did some management development work with Qualcomm, a U.S.-based telecommunications company, I started one presentation with a saying etched in large print on the wall of the gymnasium of my kid's school. "Tell me, I forget. Show me, I remember. Involve me, I understand."

If we take this bit of old wisdom at face value, we can see it is a process that requires completion. We move from the introduction of "telling" through to the culmination of "involving," and by doing so, bring people to "understanding."

This progression, this learning and understanding curve, if you will, once codified and clearly expressed in the mission, the vision, the policies, and the training materials of the organization, takes root and becomes second nature to us. It takes root in the blended soil of these tasks, with every part of the organization involved, taking the lead in some areas and a supporting role in others. In essence, we learn about the rule of three like Figure 6.2 and we think about it like Figure 6.3.

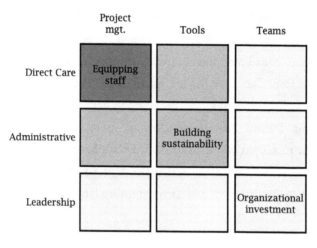

Figure 6.2

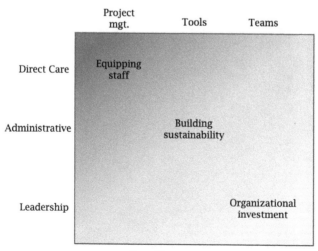

Figure 6.3

## Ready to Go

In Part Two we have addressed each part of our big question: "Who does what and how?" With the Trauma Responsive Care rule of three as our road map and equipped with our lessons for managing change from Part One, we are ready to go. The next part of the book is a step-by-step guide. Because the steps laid out for implementing Trauma Responsive Care are more detailed, the information presented will expand on what we have discussed so far. Remember, however, as you follow the steps, you can always thumb back through Parts One and Two to regain a larger perspective.

## part three

## When? A Step-by-Step Guide

"The art of progress is to preserve order amid change and to preserve change amid order."

—Alfred North Whitehead[102]

"It has

To construct a new stage. It has to be on that stage
And, like an insatiable actor, slowly and
With meditation, speak words that in the ear,
In the delicatest ear of the mind, repeat ..."

—Wallace Stevens[103]

The rest of this book is a step-by-step guide to implementing Trauma Responsive Care. There are eight steps presented in three chapters.

As a step-by-step guide, it is relatively brief, and each step is as concrete and focused as possible. I would like to say it's as simple as starting with Step One, and then moving on to Step Two and so forth. There are a couple of problems with this, however. First, although the steps are generally sequential, the process is more complex. You don't, for instance, necessarily have to finish one step to move on to the next, and some steps will be going on concurrently. That's why skilled project management is such an important component to this process.

Second, it's hard to keep track of all the various action steps under way as well as master some understanding of the lessons for managing change and the interplay between the various components that make up the rule of three. You will find it helpful to have access to a broader, deeper discussion of concepts involved in each step.

To help with this, I have provided some basic information with each action step and where in the previous chapters, in Parts One and Two, you can find the relevant information.

Each action step is labeled with:
- The action step itself
- The dominant sector of the organization involved with the action step, the *Who* of the organization (Chapter Four)
- The general task of the action step, the *What* of implementing (Chapter Five)
- The dominant strategy involved in the action step, the *How* of implementing (Chapter Six)
- The relevant lessons for managing change (Chapter Two)
- Discussion of the action step

You will also find it helpful to occasionally go back to Chapter Three and reorient yourself and other leaders in your organization with the guiding principles and the foundations of Trauma Responsive Care, especially in the early steps of this chapter on getting started.

One last warning: Don't let perfection be the enemy of the good.[104] This is like learning a language; you learn by trying and getting it not quite right, then getting it a bit better. Remember the four R's and the last of our eight lessons: Evaluate continually. Keep moving.

## chapter seven

## Getting Started: Steps 1, 2 & 3

The first three action steps set the stage and get things rolling. They start exclusively with executive leadership but end with garnering middle management buy-in and investment.

**Step 1:** Organize your team and prepare for change
**Dominant Sector, Who (Chapter Four):** Executive leadership
**General Task, What (Chapter Five):** Organizational investment
**Dominant Strategy, How (Chapter Six):** Project management, teams
**Relevant Lessons (Chapter Two):**
    Lesson One: Communicate
    Lesson Two: Build a sense of urgency
    Lesson Three: Create a vision
**Discussion:**
This first step starts when the senior management team truly commits to implementing a trauma-responsive environment. There are four major tasks to be done before a launch. They are:

- **Build the infrastructure for change.** This is identifying a project manager and, let me sound formal here, vesting this project manager with the responsibility and authority to form and support the three teams that will be operational during the change:

~ A resource team, concerned with equipping and supporting all staff. This includes tracking training to make sure everyone is trained, building a training for new staff, and building a structure for refresher training.

~ A sustainability team, concerned with creating and coordinating activities around the four R's of Chapter Five (see Action Step Six).

~ An organizational investment team, concerned with institutionalizing the change through reviewing and changing all written materials like value statements, policies and procedures, and training materials (see Action Step Seven).

Here's a helpful hint: Depending on your own organization's characteristics, size, and structure, the number and size of the teams may vary. We worked with one very small agency of about twenty staff members. The executive director and her assistant did all this work, bringing in the occasional DSP on specific activities. You may use a large team that breaks into smaller groups for each task, or you may combine, say, the concerns of building sustainability and organizational investment into a single team. Be creative and make the structure work for you.

- **Forge the message that introduces the move to Trauma Responsive Care, carrying a palpable sense of urgency.** Obviously, this includes getting buy-in from everyone on the senior management team. But moving forward does not have to wait for this. To borrow a military concept, this is a maneuvered advance, not an advance of attrition. There may be that senior manager or department head who is a bit skeptical or just isn't as convinced or excited. Remember Lesson Five: Nurture change where it grows (instead of worrying about where it isn't growing). The most important thing is that the repeated message to everyone at the start clearly conveys the need to change:

~ We are not doing the best we can for the people we support and here's why ...

~ We have got to do better for the people we support. We have to be part of their healing from trauma and not be a barrier to it ...

~ We are not living up to our own mission, and that changes today ...

The information in Chapter One, "Why should an agency try to be responsive to trauma?" may help you develop and articulate this sense of urgency and grapple with how to communicate it.

• **Create the vision for the future.** The first actions of preparing the way must include a clear vision of the future. This is not a list of things the organization will do. There is a place for that, to be sure, but first senior management must create that captivating story, clearly stating what your world will look like when you're done: "We are doing our part; we are part of the healing; we are truly living out our mission."

Review the guiding principles and the foundations of Trauma Responsive Care in Chapter Three, "The Nature of *This* Change." This chapter will be helpful as you work to articulate your own vision of a new future.

• **Start thinking about outcomes.** When your leadership team discusses the vision, you're at the cusp of talking about outcomes. Don't shy away from it. The best outcomes to track, to document potential positive impact from Trauma Responsive Care, are outcomes you already track, like the number of incidences of violence or the number of times staff resorted to a restriction or restraint of some kind. You may also think about positive impact on retention, thus decreasing turnover. Remember, though, these are outcomes, not outputs, like the number of people trained or reported use of one or more CALMER Skills, though you may also track those for a time. We start the discussion of outcomes here and prepare for trial and error and refinement. We will come back to outcomes later.

All four of these actions are discussed in senior management meetings and are reflected in the minutes. All three discussions result in something tangible: a document, an assignment, a rough list, a small initial change to a budget line — something. This is the beginning of institutionalizing the change.

**Step 2:** Get your bearings: Assess your organization
**Dominant Sector, Who (Chapter Four):** Executive leadership
**General Task, What (Chapter Five):** Organizational investment
**Dominant Strategy, How (Chapter Six):** Project management and the organizational investment team
**Relevant Lessons (Chapter Two):**
  Lesson One: Communicate
  Lesson Seven: Institutionalize the Change
**Discussion:**
There is one major task in this step: Assess your organization.

Assessing your organization is a process of evaluating or judging its readiness or fitness. We are most familiar with this process in the form of a regulatory or certification review, where our policies and practices are judged against a preexisting standard. An assessment is always relative to something. Even a general assessment framework like the classic SWOT[105] analysis quite specifically assesses the organization's competitive position in its own market. In this step, you are assessing your organization relative to a trauma-responsive environment.

When you think about how to assess your organization, you probably think first about a tool or a framework. There are some trauma-informed organizational assessments out there, though very few tailored to the I/DD sector.[106] A good tool can be quite helpful and make this process much easier, but it's not strictly necessary. Also, more and more, various certifications and accreditations are becoming "trauma-informed" and can help provide a framework for assessing the organization.

Whether you use a tool or build your own framework, there are a few things to keep in mind:

- The focus of the assessment is on trauma-responsive practices and organizational habits. Eventually, it will become a valuable part of your overall strategic planning, but at the beginning, don't let it get bigger than this until you're ready.
- As discussed above, there are two sides to the organization: the hard, written side and the soft, cultural side. You have to assess both. If, for example, you are assessing training, look at what your staff receives now and what they use (soft side), as well as the materials used in training (hard side). Incidentally, any goals that emerge from this will also reflect both sides — newly

developed materials for training (hard) and what staff takes away, remembers, and applies (soft).

- The first goal of the assessment is to help with building sustainability, reminding, reinforcing, refining, and repeating.
- The second goal is to help with organizational investment by providing a checklist (or at least a framework) for doing the work of institutionalizing the change into practice and into policy, training materials, and any other written expression of the organization.

To do this thoroughly enough to be useful, you need to address six main areas:

- Physical safety
- The gathering and use of trauma-related customer information
- Management style and practices
- Practices of hiring, training, and supporting staff
- Collaborative practices
- Policies and procedures

Since you are gathering information on a wide variety of items, you will have to employ a variety of methods, like reviewing policies and procedures and other written materials. You may also interview individual staff or hold focus group interviews to get at staff opinion and perspective.

And, as you know your agency well, you will be able to cut corners and check something off without confirming because you already know you do this or that. Don't! You need to put on a "veil of ignorance"[107] and act as if you don't know. I know in my own experience in running an agency or doing policy I would report with certainty that a given subject was addressed in policy "x," only to realize later that this policy didn't quite say what I remembered it saying.

Ideally, the assessment will leave you with a map for systematically codifying Trauma Responsive Care throughout all the documents that inform the world of what you do and how you think about it, as well as actually impacting what you do and how you think about it. This map should provide a clear path to the alignment discussed in Chapter One — where our mission aligns with customer needs. This in turn aligns with the value to the customer we present and our demonstration of that value. All of this is based on staff equipped and ready to provide that value.

In the first step, we discussed forming teams as part of the infrastructure of implementing Trauma Responsive Care. Here is the first instance of using one of those teams. The organizational investment team actually does the assessment.[108] Since this team focuses on institutionalizing the various parts of the change to Trauma Responsive Care, it should be tilted toward senior management positions — people who can easily take on the responsibility and authority to review and propose changes to policy.

This action step results in a document that can be shared and refined and ultimately becomes a working document — further institutionalizing the change to Trauma Responsive Care.

**Step Three:** Get middle-management buy-in and energize frontline supervisors

**Dominant Sector, Who (Chapter Four):** Executive leadership and administrative staff

**General Task, What (Chapter Five):** Building sustainability

**Dominant Strategy, How (Chapter Six):** Project management and the sustainability team

**Relevant Lessons (Chapter Two):**

> Lesson One: Communicate
>
> Lesson Four: Rely on Persuasion
>
> Lesson Five: Nurture Change Where It Grows
>
> Lesson Six: Grab Short-Term Wins and Leverage Them

**Discussion:**

In this last action step of getting started, leadership tests their work of building a sense of urgency and creating a vision as they work to get the buy-in of managers and energize frontline supervisors.

This buy-in is essential, so keep working at it until you feel some traction. You are relying on persuasion (Lesson Four), to convince middle management of the need for change as well as what the change entails. Be sure not to overwhelm people, but make any amount of information available as they want. This is not a need-to-know situation. Discuss reasons, methods, information — everything — but always come back to the need to implement and the vision for the future.

This is where that vision must catch fire, so to speak. Remember to nurture the flame where it sparks and don't worry so much about where it hasn't seemed to catch (Lesson Five). This is also when you start gathering stories that helped create buy-in (Lesson Six) and start refining and repeating them.

How do you do this? There are a number of possibilities. It can be a training/discussion or a series of discussions. If possible, consider holding a management retreat, off-site, and use the event as a kickoff. This can be hard to do, so you may need to do a few events to make it easy for most to participate — but not too easy. When some miss, urging those who attend to "catch their colleagues up" will foster conversation.

When the Houses of Parliament in London were damaged in bombing raids in World War II, many thought this a great opportunity to enlarge the structure, already too small to hold all its members comfortably. Prime Minister Winston Churchill insisted they be restored exactly how they were and not be expanded. His reasoning: In important matters of state, the august and crowded chamber, when everyone was in session, would amplify a sense of urgency and importance.

Creating that sense of urgency is not just in what you do, but in how you do it.

Although there may be written materials — training materials, handouts, or a PowerPoint presentation — the bulk of the impact here is in the hearts and minds of the administrative and management staff. This is squarely in the task of building sustainability and is perfect for a team approach concentrating on this task.

......................................................................................................

## chapter eight

## Equip Your Staff: Steps 4 & 5

The next two action steps, Steps Four and Five, bridge the three tasks of equipping staff with efforts to ramp things up and impact the short-term, soft side of the organizations, by beginning to build sustainability.

**Step Four:** Training, Training, and Training

**Dominant Sector, Who (Chapter Four):** Direct Support Professionals

**General Task, What (Chapter Five):** Equipping staff

**Dominant Strategy, How (Chapter Six):** Project management and the resource team

**Relevant Lessons (Chapter Seven):**

　　Lesson One: Communicate

　　Lesson Four: Rely on Persuasion

　　Lesson Five: Nurture Change Where It Grows

　　Lesson Six: Grab Short-Term Wins and Leverage Them

**Discussion:**

Let's deal with the toughest question first. Even more than with the organizational assessment, the training questions make us confront one of the most basic decisions in any business: Do we build or buy? Making this decision requires a balance of resources unique to every organization and is beyond the scope of this book. Whether you build your own curriculum or hire someone to build it and train your staff, two things are essential. First, the curriculum must be based on Trauma Responsive Care as presented in Palay's *The Way Through: Trauma Responsive Care for Intellectual and Developmental Disability Professionals*.[109] Palay discusses the brain science behind Trauma Responsive Care and established the importance of human connection, joining the fundamental elements of trauma-informed care, feeling safe, and feeling some sense of control. This is what makes Trauma Responsive Care so unique and so powerful — safe, connected, and in control applied as a universal precaution. In Chapter Three, I presented the guiding principles and the foundations of Trauma Responsive Care. Combined with the implementation strategies of this book, Trauma Responsive Care is a potent tool for change into a sustainably trauma-responsive environment. We will discuss this in more detail below.

Second, the project manager must coordinate the development of the training and not just roll it out. Having a single point of coordination will make it much easier to be sure you get exactly what you need for your organization. The rest of this discussion will develop the parameters within which the actual curriculum must rest and the job it must do to fully equip your staff.

As a systems approach, Trauma Responsive Care is built around vehicles that have strength as replicators and transmitters of both ideas and values. Through the training, for example, something as easily remembered as the phrase "safe, connected, and in control," carries a powerful sense of mission, value, and empathy into every interaction. To accomplish this so the whole *system* works, the training given to staff must meet three essential conditions:

- The training must be research-based and must carry a distinct sense of urgency. It must take into consideration, as much as is practical, the latest research into trauma and how it impacts the people we support. The strength of helping someone feel safe, connected, and in control, and the power of healing contained in the action, are steeped in research. That connection must be maintained.

- The training must focus primarily on the staff, the people who do the work of the organization. Further, the training must help staff prepare for their work and focus on what they can do to help someone feel safe, connected, and in control. This is not a treatment imposed on the people we support; this is what we bring to the interaction.

- Given the tasks that emerge from the first two, the training must provide concrete actions or skills for staff to help people feel safe, connected, and in control. Practicing these skills consistently over time must prove effective tools to help people self-regulate and to help them feel safe, connected, and in control. Moreover, these skills must be effective as real-time interventions powerful enough to have an immediate calming effect. These are the CALMER Skills.

Trauma Responsive Care fills these conditions. As you adapt Palay's book and the contents of Chapter Three of this book into a curriculum, take care that these essentials translate into your training materials.

This action step has three parts: training current staff, constructing training for new staff as they join the organization, and building refresher training to keep the concepts alive over the long term.

Here are some concrete strategies alluded to in Chapter Four.

- First of all, construct a curriculum you can use for new staff just coming on board and put it in place.
- Second, hold special trainings, with some fanfare, using the same curriculum, for current staff to get close to 60% trained — that critical mass discussed in Chapter Four.
- Track the staff who attend and direct the remaining 40% to sign up for a Trauma Responsive Care session offered to new staff through the onboarding process. This basic "two birds, one stone" strategy will cut the amount of time and effort it takes to get all current staff trained all while onboarding new staff fully trained. The same curriculum can be abbreviated into a refresher class.
- Build this abbreviated class around the concept of Trauma Responsive Care as an emotional universal precaution and couple it with Standard First Aid's universal precaution in injury treatment. Coupling the two applications of "universal precaution" will increase the impact of both.

Obviously, the tracking element of implementing training is perfect for a project manager. On the other hand, the larger task of adapting a curriculum out of *The Way Through* is a task for the resource team mentioned in the very first action step. If not already formed and ready to go, this task of developing and thoroughly understanding a curriculum, requiring a team approach, is where the resource team earns its chops.

In the next step, the resource team begins to function as a brain trust of sorts, supporting a workforce just getting used to thinking first and foremost about helping the people they support — and one another — feel safe, connected, and in control. Spending time translating Palay's work into an in-house curriculum is a necessary part of this journey. Everything is interconnected.

The outcome of this work is the long-term backbone of organizational investment, concrete training materials, not to mention policies and procedures for using them. The fanfare I mentioned around the initial push also overlaps with the next action step.

**Step Five:** Developing resources and the people who manage them: the resource team

**Dominant Sector, Who (Chapter Four):** Administrative staff

**General Task, What (Chapter Five):** Building sustainability and organizational investment

**Dominant Strategy, How (Chapter Six):** Teams

**Relevant Lessons (Chapter Two):**

   Lesson One: Communicate

   Lesson Five: Nurture Change Where It Grows

   Lesson Six: Grab Short-Term Wins and Leverage Them

   Lesson Seven: Institutionalize the Change

**Discussion:**

Earlier I said that although these actions steps appear sequential, they often overlap and are always interconnected. This action step is a case in point. This step of developing the resource team starts in Step Four — developing a curriculum out of Palay's work, for training staff in Trauma Responsive Care that fits your organization. This is, in a real sense, a school for the resource team. And this education is important because this team is the central core of Trauma Responsive Care.

In my consulting work, I have found myself frequently using the phrase, "Every temple needs a priest." What this means is simple. If any given *system,* anything from an informal loose way of doing something to a full-blown information system, like a software package, is critical to the organization's functioning, the organization must make sure it is someone's job to know the system, where it came from, and why you have it. This is the subtle, long-term driver of sustainability.

There's an old story of a child making the large family pot roast for the first time, following an old family recipe. She gets to the step where the ends of the roast are trimmed off and stops. She goes to her mother and asks why the ends must be trimmed off? "That's the way I was taught by my mother," she says. The little chef goes to her grandmother and asks the same question. "I don't know; that's how I was taught by my mother." The girl calls her great-grandmother and asks. At this question, her great-grandmother laughs and says, "Because otherwise the roast wouldn't fit in my pot."

In the long run, someone has to know that we trim the roast so it fits in the pot. And so, when we get a larger pot, someone will be able to adapt our recipe.

In implementing Trauma Responsive Care, the resource team becomes institutional memory. It is the backbone of innovation and the lifeblood of sustainability. Of the three teams we discuss in these action steps, the resource team is the most important because it lasts the longest, it overlaps the most with the activities of the other teams, and it is most dependent on learning the lessons of managing change.[110]

Beyond training materials, which overlaps with the tasks of organizational investment, the resource team should identify and create resources where they are needed to respond to trauma more effectively. In our work with agencies over almost a decade, we have identified two areas of vulnerability the team should focus on as the training initiative referred to above winds down and you have close to a critical mass trained. These are support for those difficult to support and support for those in crisis.

- **Support for those difficult to support.** If I were inviting you over for chili tonight (just a few of you at a time, of course), I would go to the grocery store and get what I need and then make the chili. Although my chili changes from time to time, I make it a lot and so can adapt easily and quickly. If, on the other hand, we decided to have duck à l'orange with black truffles and a crème brûlée for dessert, I would write the ingredients down and take the list and the recipe with me to the grocery store. It's harder than chili, less familiar, and more complicated, so I need tools to help me with the task, like a shopping list and a recipe. I will also need practice, so next time you come over, it will be better still.

  It's the same concept here. When you think about helping people feel safe, connected, and in control, you can probably think of someone with whom this would be relatively easy. It may even come naturally. With others, however, those struggling with known and obvious trauma, or those with complex needs or struggling with behavioral or emotional issues, this task of helping them feel safe, connected, and in control may be more difficult. And so, you may need a tool, like a form or a worksheet, to help you do it. Whatever tool or process you come up with, there are some basic components you should cover:

1. Make sure your tool or process starts, as much as possible, with a clear understanding of the person and what people like about them.

2. Then, review how the person reacts to fear. Remember that a lot of the time, emotions like anger are masking deeper emotions like fear or shame.[111]

3. Your tool or process should also list and discuss the CALMER Skills that provide the best response.

4. It is also important to help the person retell their own story by helping them identify and recognize their own strengths and what people like about them. This is not just reframing. The things people enjoy about the person, their abiding character strengths,[112] are essential elements of helping them retell their own story.

- **Support for those in crisis.** Your agency probably already has guidelines or a protocol for responding to an emerging or full-blown crisis. This is a good starting point. But as Trauma Responsive Care shifts our thinking on disruptive behavior from actions of belligerence or defiance to possible modes of communicating fear, these guidelines and protocols will need to be adjusted. A new approach must be based in brain science. The top priority, therefore, is to help the person feel safe and in control through caring and supportive connection. Remember, none of us can think about or analyze alternative responses to fear while our brain is telling our whole body we are not safe. Try doing long division while the bear is closing in on you.[113]

These are not easy tasks and take a lot of time, trial, and error to get it right. You've heard it said that anything worth doing is worth doing right. In this endeavor, you should also remember G.K. Chesterton's insight, "If a thing is worth doing, it is worth doing badly."[114] You can't wait to do this until you can do it perfectly. If you wait for perfection, you'll never do it.

## chapter nine

# The Long Game: Steps 6, 7 & 8

**Step Six:** Building Sustainability: The Four R's

**Dominant Sector, Who (Chapter Four):** Administrative staff

**General Task, What (Chapter Five):** Building sustainability

**Dominant Strategy, How (Chapter Six):** Teams, the sustainability team

**Relevant Lessons (Chapter Seven):**

   Lesson One: Communicate

   Lesson Two: Build a Sense of Urgency

   Lesson Three: Create a Vision

   Lesson Four: Rely on Persuasion

   Lesson Five: Nurture Change Where It Grows

   Lesson Six: Grab Short-Term Wins and Leverage Them

**Discussion:**

As you recall, the task of building sustainability addresses the soft side of the organization. There are many ways to think about this soft side. It's the organization's personality, its feel. It encompasses everything from the vibe you get at the main office to the attitudes of the staff. We usually describe this overarching "ghost in the machine"[115] as the corporate culture, that ganglia of connected perceptions, attitudes, and values — how the organization thinks and feels about itself and how it confronts challenges and makes decisions. The work involved in building sustainability seeks to impact these perceptions, attitudes, and values.

I have also referred to this task of building sustainability as focused on the short term. If you think about diverting the flow of a river to stop erosion, you can imagine placing a large permanent structure, like a wall that adjusts the flow of the current and stops the erosion. First, you need temporary means to get the current moving in the right direction and also out of the way, so to speak, so you can place the permanent wall. Here we are talking about those temporary, short-term strategies. The sustainability team builds those temporary practices while the more permanent work of organizational investment is completed.

This is accomplished through the four R's — remember, reinforce, remind, and repeat — and the activities of the four R's are managed by the sustainability team. Think about this as a big internal ad campaign. We've been through the training, and now, as we get the long-term changes in place, remember, we are doing something new. We reinforce and refine this "something new" by discussing and grappling with it.

Here are some strategies you can employ for each of these R's:

### Remember or Remind
- Memes in posters, emails, tweets, etc.
- Agenda items for standing team or area meetings
- Announcements of events, additional trainings, etc.
- Print business card-sized reminders and spread them around

### Reinforce
- Gather and repeat stories of using the CALMER Skills

- Persuade senior and middle management to open conversations with their staff by asking, "How can I help you feel safe, connected, and in control today?" This sounds corny, but that's the point — exaggerated, tongue in cheek, it doesn't matter — it reinforces the concept and has a subtle power to change perceptions.
- Have T-shirts made and give them out as prizes to reinforce "responsive moments."

### Refine

- Host discussions of the CALMER Skills in action — both successes and perceived flops. This is how we learn, by doing it badly at first.
- Ask staff to identify moments when a particular skill worked well, or challenge them to identify their favorite.
- Dedicate a section in the newsletter to discuss how Trauma Responsive Care works in the "real world" — complete with guest contributors from all parts of the organization.

### Repeat

- All of the above — refresh.

How long do these short-term efforts go on? Obviously it varies, but the first big wave should be about three to six months. One of the biggest variables is the work of the organizational investment team. As revised mission and value statements come online,[116] the initial work of building sustainability begins to wane.

However, after the initial push, you still have work to do, and it never really ends. With this constant refreshing and revitalizing, we are more in the realm of general organizational best practices. Let me illustrate. I ran a subsidiary of a large national organization in which all of the companies surveyed employees every other year. We asked, among other things, if staff knew the mission statement and knew what it meant. We also asked if staff knew the story of the organization's name, something that carried value for the company. Through this survey, we regularly found that we needed to reinforce these concepts. The fast-paced nature of the work, turnover, and time passing had eroded these things, and we needed to make our deeper purpose, our reason for being, more explicit and relevant. If Trauma Responsive Care is to become truly sustainable, it has to be constantly monitored and reinforced. In this way, the work of the sustainability team becomes diffused into standard management practices, but these practices must now be steeped in the values of being truly responsive to the trauma or potential trauma of everyone connected to the organization. And this overlaps with and merges into the work of the organizational investment team.

**Step 7:** Play the long game: building organizational investment
**Dominant Sector, Who (Chapter Four):** Executive leadership
**General Task, What (Chapter Five):** Organizational investment
**Dominant Strategy, How (Chapter Six):** Teams, the organizational investment team
**Relevant Lessons (Chapter Seven):**
   Lesson One: Communicate
   Lesson Three: Create a Vision
   Lesson Seven: Institutionalize the Change
   Lesson Eight: Evaluate Continually
**Discussion:**
Remember that imaginary river from our previous action step — that permanent wall we have to place to make sure the river stays

on its new course while not eroding the banks? The work of the organizational investment team is to codify or institutionalize our change to Trauma Responsive Care — to put that permanent, flow-guiding wall in place.

The organizational investment team started its work with the organizational assessment in the first action step. Also in that first action step, the first iteration of the organizational investment team was senior management working to build the infrastructure for sustained change. The organizational investment team formed in that step must still retain senior management involvement because it is concerned with work that mandates senior management input and authority, namely, creating and changing written aspects of institutional functioning and memory.

The work of the organizational investment team is straightforward. Taking the guiding principles and foundations of Trauma Responsive Care and its basic components — helping everyone feel safe, connected, and in control as a universal precaution — as a backdrop, the team must review all relevant policies, procedures, training materials, and forms, including the values and mission statements, and make sure they actively support responsiveness to trauma.

That's a big, long, complicated sentence. (My editor had a bit of a problem with it. She called it run-on, can you imagine?) You've probably already realized that it all boils down to four words: Review all relevant policies.

What is relevant? Let's look at the extremes to help us figure this out. If you have, for instance, written guidance on how to decide between purchasing or leasing a copier, you're probably safe not to worry about reviewing this one. On the other hand, a policy that structures on-call schedules for frontline managers is definitely relevant. Why? It's a management procedure that informs crisis response and managerial oversite after hours but is not directly related to actual support of the people served. That's true, but the way you do it now might inadvertently lead to higher rates of burnout or diminished judgment. Reviewing this policy while asking the question, "How can this policy help the on-call supervisor feel safe, connected, and in control?" can alleviate an unseen corrosive agent on quality.

Along those same lines, consider this: An agency working through policy from a trauma-responsive perspective initially determined that its vacation request policy was not relevant to review. Later in the process, they revisited this decision. The policy required a two-week notice for vacation time. This allowed management to plan for the absence of the vacationing staff — perfectly valid. The team began to feel it would be more responsive if staff could use their vacation time in smaller bits with shorter notification time. They ended up recommending changes. If you take this a little further, you can imagine the team recommending a complete overhaul of the policy in favor of combining everything into a paid time off system in order to meet valid managerial planning needs while maximizing responsiveness to staff needs.

Even with this discussion and these examples, it may not be very clear at first and the organizational investment team may have difficulty sorting everything out. That's okay. Trust the process and it will become easier for the team to do its work with practice.

In our river analogy, the building sustainability team creates that short-term perceptive and attitudinal change while the organizational investment team builds the policies and procedures that will govern the long-term direction of the organization. Organizations cannot stop doing everything else in order to devote all of their time to reviewing policies. This takes time and patience, and this time should be taken so you get it right, maybe by getting it slightly wrong along the way. Ultimately, the work of the organizational investment team will make or break the long-term success of the change through the process of institutionalization. Once Trauma Responsive Care is invested into the structure of the organization, the sheer power of the organization itself will produce its own sustainable momentum to further solidify the change.[117]

**Step 8:** Don't forget outcomes

**Dominant Sector, Who (Chapter Four):** Executive leadership

**General Task, What (Chapter Five):** Organizational investment

**Dominant Strategy, How (Chapter Six):** Teams and project management

**Relevant Lessons (Chapter Seven):**

Lesson One: Communicate

Lesson Seven: Institutionalize the Change

Lesson Eight: Evaluate Continually

**Discussion:**

There is a bit of British wartime propaganda originally developed by the rather secretive Ministry of Information[118] that has resonated so well in the last decade or so as a meme of resolve and steadfastness, that it is highly likely you know it and you might even know someone with a T-shirt or mug brandishing it: "Keep Calm and Carry On." In the 1940s, it felt wonderfully British, and these days it has become so ubiquitous that it models a trait we all strive to instill in ourselves and others in times of prolonged struggle. This is exactly what it was supposed to do at the time of its creation.

As I have said a few times in this book, this task is long and diffi-cult, so you must be steadfast and approach it with great resolve. And, as this book is all about, break it down into manageable chunks. One of the best ways to both grab the power of the orga-nization and to fast-track institutionalization is through measuring outputs and outcomes.

What's the difference? Outputs are the things you do to accom-plish the goal, and the outcome is accomplishing the goal. Here's a quick example. We want staff to help people feel safe, connected, and in control. So, we train them. We teach them the concept (safe, connected, and in control) and we teach them methods (the CALMER Skills). In this effort, the output is the training. The outcome is a staff that routinely employs the CALMER Skills to help people feel safe, connected, and in control. We measure the outputs (number of trainings and people trained), and we measure the outcomes (the extent to which staff are using the CALMER Skills and helping people feel safe, connected, and in control and, more to the point, what happens when they do). Both have their place, and both are important. Let's start with outputs.

In the case of Trauma Responsive Care, you must codify, in policy and practice, the things you will do to become and stay responsive to trauma. These outputs are mostly the things you have done thus far in the initiative to change to Trauma Responsive Care along with the things you do to make sure your commitment does not erode and you don't slowly move away from it. The most important and most obvious is refresher training you couple with Standard First Aid so physical and emotional universal precautions are retrained at the same time. You need to add this, explicitly, to your policies covering training.

There are two other policy-based structural changes you should consider.

- **Continuing sustainability.** You should create a policy that expresses commitment to sustaining and supporting Trauma Responsive Care with staff. This policy should:

  ~ Assign responsibility to produce regular events, drives, or activities to recreate and deepen agency commitment to Trauma Responsive Care. This can be a standing team with rotating membership, or it can be attached to the activities of an existing support unit like training or quality management. Here's a helpful hint, though: Keep it out of human resources. They should be involved but not responsible for it. They have too much going on already.

  ~ Codify a loose schedule. Don't leave it wide open with language like "shall, when needed," but don't make it too rigid. Think of something in between, such as two to four events, drives, actions, etc., a year.

  ~ Don't depend too much on the same event year after year. Change what you do and be creative. If something works well, be mindful of that and use that strategy again, but be ready for the steam to run out and move on to something else.

- **Continuous policy review.** Many agencies already have something like this in place. Thou shalt review agency policies on a given schedule so everything is reviewed every five years or so. Most states have something like this in statute to make sure administrative rule is reviewed regularly. If you don't, create it. If you do, change it to include an explicit commitment to

Trauma Responsive Care. This policy could also mandate the identification of policy content that should explicitly reflect a trauma-responsive commitment, like training or crisis intervention, for example.

These three policy changes — on training, actions to sustain commitment, and actions to review policies regularly — create the backbone of policy-based outputs to support and sustain your institutional commitment to Trauma Responsive Care. Now, let's look at outcomes.

In the beginning, don't worry about adding outcomes. You probably already measure the important things you need to measure to make sure your various control systems are working. In clinical and operational areas, you most likely measure things like the number of "unusual incidents" and "major unusual incidents" or the like. You probably also measure things like medication errors or other lapses in health-related treatment regimes. In staffing, you probably already measure turnover and the impact of efforts to improve retention. Start with these by charting them over time and marking with a line the milestones of implementing Trauma Responsive Care (see an example in Figure 9.1[119]).

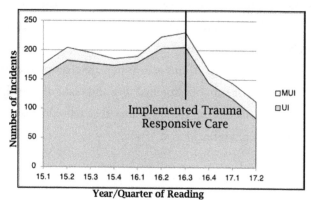

Figure 9.1

New milestones, like an event or action to bolster the effort, produce new marks so you can see the impact of the output on the outcome.

Another reason to start with what we have is that we are driven by the various processes, outputs, and outcomes that directly impact us. So, for example, processes and measures of quality that regulators or accreditation reviewers look at are usually a higher priority and take up more of our attention than measures of quality that regulators don't examine.

So, we protect ourselves from eroding commitment, turnover, and strained institutional memory by injecting Trauma Responsive Care into the policies, procedures, outcomes, and habits that already work for us.

Eventually, if you don't already do it, you should add processes of regularly gathering input from both staff and customers and make sure you ask questions that will allow you to judge knowledge and use of the concepts and skills employed to support a trauma-responsive environment. Then you will have operational outcomes (e.g., decreased number of incidents, increased retention, and decreased absenteeism), as well as more perception-based outcomes (e.g., improved staff knowledge and morale and higher customer and stakeholder satisfaction).

The important things in this action step are creating the policy-based outputs that support sustainability and codifying the habits of seeking and measuring the outcomes that tell you that you're moving in the right direction.

## chapter ten

An Epilogue in Two Parts: How to Make Friends and Influence Policymakers

"I am about to do a new thing;

 now it springs forth, do you not perceive it?"

— Isaiah, 43:19a[120]

In 2019, an agency in Great Britain called What Works for Children's Social Care launched the Happier, Healthier Professionals research project. The idea was to find, through practical research, what programs, ideas, or activities actually made a positive difference in the emotional well-being of social workers. One intervention they developed and tested through 2019 and 2020 was "symbolic reward." Researchers gathered a baseline on personal well-being and then had bosses send a personalized letter of thanks to their social work staff. Then they surveyed again in a month. They found that the treatment group reported higher levels of "subjective well-being" and were more motivated. They also reported feeling a stronger sense of belonging and a stronger sense of "social worth." They even missed work slightly less than the control group.[121]

There are a few recent studies like this, covering a number of industries, that look at some form of being nice or showing personal appreciation in intangible, non-financial ways.[122] Two things stand out just from the nature of the experiments and findings in terms of improved well-being and a sense of belonging to and being a part of the organization's mission. The first is that it has to be personal. An impersonal form letter of general appreciation does not make the cut. The second thing, related to the first, is that it has to be genuine.

In other words, being nice and showing your appreciation has a positive impact on your staff and their performance only if you really are nice and really do appreciate them. And to think we needed studies to tell us this! Good managers do not thrive on managerial skills alone. They like people; they like *their* people. I don't know how to form this into a skill for managers or as an item on a "good manager checklist." Maybe something like this: Know the people who work for you and genuinely like them.[123]

It all comes down to a manager's ability to motivate their staff, to get the most out of them, while at the same time providing them the support they need to keep happy and healthy and therefore productive. This is not barking out an order: "You will be happy in your work!" This is the much more subtle art of influencing. This is the stuff of leadership.

I want to end this book with a two-part look at this art of influencing as part, perhaps the final and ongoing part, of implementing Trauma Responsive Care. The first part focuses inward and looks at leadership habits that will serve any leader well and are close to essential for a trauma-responsive environment. The second part will look outward at actions and habits that will help us influence policymakers.

## Influencing Inwardly: Good Habits for Managers

By their nature, most how-to books on management are quite general, because the practice of management is so diverse and vast. At the same time, the particulars of any given industry are still important. So, you can often read hundreds of pages for a relatively small payoff of insight. This is not a condensed version of general management knowledge or an oversimplified list of "things to do" (although I will talk about some things to do). Rather it is a short gathering of management and leadership values that are pretty basic yet have a reverberating impact. I call them habits because they all contain a necessary element of effort to change your outlook — you have to work at them and develop them.

Throughout this book, we've discussed each part of the organization and where it is most heavily involved in implementing Trauma Responsive Care. We've learned that a significant part of this venture is consumed with things like cajoling and reminding and convincing and refining. This is done through trainings and organized discussions — things that you as "manager" arrange and make happen. But it is also done through quick conversations, pep talks, words of encouragement, and through suggestions on how to handle something, giving guidance, and even asking for guidance. This is the bread and butter of leadership, and persistence here will win the day in creating a truly trauma-responsive environment, no matter how difficult it proves to be and in almost any corporate culture.[124]

These habits should, first of all, call our attention back to the guiding principles of Trauma Responsive Care, especially the first — that what we really do is develop and maintain supportive and caring relationships with people. The guiding principles and the foundations of Trauma Responsive Care inform our view of things generally and provide us with the perspectives through which we do the things we do as managers. Think about them. We should also remember the CALMER Skills themselves.[125] Develop them and integrate them into your own established or emerging management style. They will serve you well in an ever-changing management and leadership climate.

### Seek to Manage Systems, Not People

The reason for this is simple. You can't manage people — not really. You can only manage the systems and processes through which they manage themselves. So, if you approach your tasks of management in this way, you'll get a lot further faster and with much less frustration. You can say to a candidate for a job, "To keep this job, you must show up at this time, stay for this long, and do (and don't do) certain things while you're here." Ultimately, though, they have to manage themselves to actually show up and do the work.

You may have heard it said that a good manager provides what their staff needs to do their work and then gets out of the way. This is, in a sense, another way of saying it. In Chapter Three, I pointed out that we are all managers — even and especially Direct Support Professionals. Day in and day out, they are called upon to manage — communicate, sometimes under duress; manage their own and others' stress; resolve conflicts; and manage shifting events, crises, and the unexpected. What they need is not directives, but a structure and the resources and support to do their work.

As a manager, you have a mixture of structure, training, guidance, and trust given to you by your bosses or your board (not to mention regulatory entities, certifying agencies, and market forces). Just so, you have to provide a mixture of structure, training, guidance, and trust to your staff through which they can manage themselves. After all, you need them to make good decisions and have sound judgment even when you're not around.

### Be Aware of How You Feel

Every decision we make, whether at work or in our personal lives, no matter how logical it may seem, is always powered by or infused with emotions — how we feel. Seemingly ordinary things like hunger, coming out of or going into a tough situation, or just plain fatigue all affect us in ways we notice and in many ways we don't necessarily notice. Studies show we have a diminished capacity for decision-making before lunch and at the end of the day. It is not uncommon for multinational companies to have policies that do not allow an executive to sign a contract within twenty-four hours of an overnight flight, out of concern for impaired judgment. So, although we like to think that we can just "think" it through, whatever it is or however we feel, it's not just our brain at work, it's all of us — our whole hungry, tired, distracted body. As philosopher Mortimer J. Adler put it, we don't think with our brain, even if we can't think without it.[126]

There are many things we can do to take better care of ourselves — eat better, get more exercise, get more and better sleep. But what can we do, in the moment, to improve our judgment and decision-making? It may sound simple, but the best thing we can do in any given moment is to be aware of how we feel. If we are aware of how we feel, we have options, we are more consciously aware of the whole situation, and we can better judge the best course of action — even if that course of action is not to make a decision right now.

This may sound familiar — it's the first three CALMER Skills.[127] Improve your awareness of how you feel by practicing these skills, as a manager, regularly — religiously — before you start work, before and during tense interactions, and before and during decision-making.

This practice will also help you get and remain calm in tense situations so you can respond as opposed to react. If I am aware that a given situation or event is making me angry, I can take a minute, I can express my emotions, or I can even postpone taking any action if circumstances allow. If I am not fully aware that a given situation or event is making me angry, then my anger is managing the situation, not me.

### Seek to Understand

You may recognize this as the first half of the fifth habit in Stephen Covey's book *Seven Habits of Highly Effective People,* first published in 1989.[128] The full habit is "seek first to understand, then to be understood." This is a good habit to have and goes along with other good habits for managers. So why just the first half? I have to admit I have this luxury because great minds before me spelled out the whole thing, but my reasons are also a little more practical. Frankly, I don't think managers need to worry too much about being understood. I think if we do better at the first part, we've got it covered. Managers naturally seek to be understood and when we are not understood, it's mostly because we speak from the outside and we don't really understand the situation.

So, we should, on a practical level, just try hard to understand — understand the situation, understand the parameters, understand the possible outcomes, and, most of all, understand, as best as we can, the perspectives and feelings of those involved, and admit it when we can't.

Now, I have used the word *practical* twice and so far it probably seems a bit general, so let's get, um, practical. How do we do this? I remember as a young child watching *The Flintstones*, an animated sitcom that followed the lives of a Stone Age family and their best friends. In one episode, Fred Flintstone was hired to fill in for a missing business tycoon because he was a dead ringer for the tycoon. Fred explained he knew nothing of running a major corporation and was told to simply repeat one of three phrases, "Whose baby is that?," "What's your angle?," and "I'll buy that." Although the following recommendations are not quite that simple, they are as close as we can get. So, when in doubt, just do these things.

- **Ask a lot of questions.** There is a bit of hidden wisdom in the fact that two of the three things Fred Flintstone was advised to say were questions. Even if you already understand and know the answer, ask anyway. Because truly understanding is not limited to an intellectual exercise of cognitive "I-get-it-ness." You have to confirm it, refine it. Understanding others and being understood is a communal activity. And as a boss, your conclusions, though they may be understood, will not be completely trusted if your people don't trust that they were truly heard.

- **Repeat the answers you receive in your own words.** This action of confirming is a two-way street. You have deepened your understanding because you've translated it into your own words. And you have communicated this understanding in an open, rather than a confrontational, way. This is now a conversation through which all involved will reach a conclusion. Not everyone will necessarily agree, but they will feel heard and understood.

- **Show your work.** This may bring back bad memories of seventh-grade math, but it's important to tell others where and how your understanding was confirmed or improved. This further solidifies the group's understanding and gives everyone yet another chance to clarify their perspective further. Just sum it all up, honestly, from your perspective: "I'm glad I asked because I thought it was different," or "I didn't fully understand this."
- **Show your appreciation.** *Please* and *thank you* are not called the magic words for nothing. Use the magic! Remember, though: You have to mean it.

Let me end with an illustration. A new executive director, taking over after an extreme crisis in quality, health, and safety that almost shut down the organization decided to ask questions. Finding no better place to start, she hosted open monthly lunches. She ordered pizza, opened the training room, and invited everyone. She told everyone, in the invitation, that these lunches were for people to come and ask questions or air problems they saw in the organization. She soon realized that for the most part, though there was some conversation, people came for the pizza and to see if anyone was dumb enough to stick their neck out. The staff had learned self-preservation well from the last administration.

So, the new boss handed out notecards and suggested people write out their question or issue and just leave it on the table when they go. One of the few early questions was this: "The handicapped parking for the office is pretty far away and down the hill. I think it ought to be closer to the front entrance."

The new boss acted quickly. She did a little research into the regulation, and within a few days of that lunch, two new temporary signs, identifying handicapped parking, in the two slots closest to the door, were erected. At the next lunch, she read the question aloud and told everyone what she learned in her research and pointed out the new signs. She also apologized for not having considered this herself and for the fact that it will take some time for new parking lines and symbols to be painted on the pavement.

She knew this was an important item, but she also knew this was a test. Through the process of the pizza and the lunches and the notecards, she bent over backward to create a dialogue and jumped on the opportunity to make it meaningful. She did not take it under advisement. She did not put it on a capital improvements list for further discussion. She acted. This, of course, was not the only new thing she did, but this action came from her desire to understand.

### Seek to Persuade, Not Coerce

Managers make decisions of various kinds and magnitudes. In fact, that's what management is all about — making decisions. And many times, managers make decisions based on incomplete information. Yet, the manager is still ultimately responsible for the decisions they make. Managers also make decisions when they do not have full control — managers, for example, have to plan for the future and, to quote Yogi Berra, "It's tough to make predictions, especially about the future."[129]

Getting in the habit of always seeking to understand naturally leads to the dynamic process of making decisions. This even applies in situations that may contain the need for corrective action, a teaching moment, if you will. "No, you're wrong," is easily understood, but it shuts everything down. The conversation is done, the connection is severed, and the learning never happens. Try something like, "I think I see what you were thinking, but let me ask, if we do (this), what do we do about (that)?" This takes longer to process, but the conversation ensues, a connection is forged, and a deeper insight on the part of the employee is much more likely to happen.

Another way to think about this is in the process of making a decision and then implementing it. If you decide on a course of action in isolation, the decision-making phase is very quick, but you are limited to your own experience. In turn, the implementation will take a long time because all of it is new to everyone. Everyone has to reinvent your process in their own minds. On the other hand, if you open the decision-making process, involving others, it will take longer, but you will benefit from the combined experience of many. In turn, implementation will be quite smooth in comparison, because everyone is already on board.

### Never Use Anger as a Means of Communication

Here is a classic story. A man is talking to his friend at the park while his child plays with some toys. The man tells the child to pack up his toys because they have to leave. He does, but then gets a few toys back out as his father is still talking with his friend. After a few minutes, the father looks down and says, "I told you to pack up; we have to go. Now do it," then goes back to his conversation. The boy keeps playing. Finally, the father yells at the child, who then packs up the remaining toys and is ready to leave.

In this story, the child had learned that the words, "Pack up, it's time to go," when stated calmly, means, "You still have time to play; we're not really leaving yet." When the words are yelled, the child can correctly decipher the communication, "Time to go." It is the emotion and not the words that carry the meaning.

I have seen many managers try to use anger or frustration, an emotion, as the primary means of communication: My staff knows it's important when I am angry. I have also seen managers seek to elicit fear on the part of staff to convey importance. This is never a good idea.

In contrast, I once worked with a manager who had specifically worked to avoid this trap. Just before I was to give a short introduction to a two-day retreat I was facilitating, he presented his division with the rather dismal numbers for the past quarter and repeated, "This is serious," in a normal tone. Because the manager had cultivated the habits of not acting out of anger and not using anger to communicate, the data and his straightforward assessment of the situation made his point. He did not need to yell. He could merely tell them he was angry at the numbers without having to demonstrate it with emotion. The message was clearer and much more effective.

Never speak or act in anger. Let your words and deeds communicate, not your emotions.

### Ramp Up Your Associative Thinking Skills

Associative thinking as a phenomenon is your brain flitting around from thought to thought, with seeming randomness and with no clear direction. It's even in the American Psychological Association's *Dictionary of Psychology*.[130] Associative thinking as a habit of thought is the honed skill of associating root concepts from one branch of knowledge or experience to another, drawing out similarities, and so gaining a deeper grasp of both sources. Like many habits of thought, it may come more naturally to some than others, but just like creativity, it is not a matter of either having it or not. It can be learned.

We all use associative thinking to some extent when we, say, use a sports analogy to explain something that is not that sport. I did exactly that in the opening chapter of this book. I used a sports story of a team that played a great game but didn't quite finish it. I used the story through analogy to develop a sense of urgency for implementing Trauma Responsive Care — we have to finish the game.

We can take it a step further, though. As a skill, it is the sharpened ability to subconsciously see related root concepts in a vast array of seemingly unrelated information or experience and apply them to solving the problem in front of you. I once talked with a manager in the automotive restoration industry who told me he'd recently realized that two of his best recent hires were two people who used to work in food service — wait staff. When he thought about it, he realized it made sense. Although it's a completely different industry, wait staff are keenly aware of their customers, and that awareness translated very well. Now, he watches for that kind of experience on applications, and restaurants are a standard recruiting ground for him. I have no idea where it came from, but I am fond of this saying: The idea for the next great topping for a sundae won't come from eating more sundaes.

How can you hone this skill? Just like learning a new musical instrument — practice.

If you've ever played a musical instrument, you know that when you are first learning, say, chords on a piano, you look at the array of notes on the sheet music and you consciously interpret the symbols, the notes, into a conscious conception of the chord C. Then you consciously form your fingers into that chord as you, still quite consciously, place your contorted hand above the appropriate keys and press. It takes two or three seconds to play the chord and you have another 499 to go in this relatively short song. After some practice, the conscious activity falls away and the note seems to skip your mind and goes straight from eye to hand. As you begin to master the song, if not the whole instrument, the notes seem to go directly from page to piano.

With practice, you might just instantaneously draw some insight from a novel you read last year and apply it to this conversation in this meeting, discussing this problem. Here are some practice drills.

- **Read.** Reading takes time and you may not have that much of it, but dedicate some of it to reading. And vary your reading and build the habit of reading more than one kind of thing — not just magazines but also books, not just nonfiction but also fiction, not just in your own field but in other fields.

- **Do things differently.** Take a different way home. Work outside. Eat something you did not like as a child and haven't eaten since. Find those built-in habits of day-to-day life that really don't matter that much and actively disrupt them.

- **Question everything.** This is not primarily a rebellious call to question authority, though it includes that. It is more an attempt to pull the weeds of assumption before they take root. One helpful mechanism is to practice the "five whys" technique. With this technique, when confronted with a problem you simply ask why, five times. This successive inquiry digs deeply into root causes and often uncovers insights just as deep.

- **Act.** Experiment with solutions on a small scale and refine them through further trial. Above all, gather input and don't be afraid to be wrong.

### INFLUENCING OUTWARDLY: QUIET, DATA-DRIVEN
### EVANGELISM — POLICYMAKERS

Obviously, the primary focus of an organization's leadership is the organization itself. And as we've discussed, this focus, across management staff, balances an emphasis on learning from the past, maximizing quality and efficiency in day-to-day operations, and planning for the future. Organizations do not operate in a vacuum, however. There are myriad market and regulatory forces at work, and many of these forces are directly impacted by policy and policymakers. So, the question emerges: How can we positively influence other providers and policymakers toward a more trauma-responsive system of care?

Let's start with where we are. The impetus behind the advances in trauma-informed care has not explicitly, we must first admit, come from the I/DD community. In fact, we were a bit late to the game. The initial drive has come from mental health and moved outward. As the concepts of trauma-informed care became more cohesive, they found their best expression in various publications of the Substance Abuse and Mental Health Services Administration (SAMHSA).[131]

Because of this, early adoption of these concepts in the I/DD community required translation and adaptation from the mental health system. In mental health services, trauma-informed concepts focused first on recognition and proper diagnosis, equipping clinicians to properly assess for and diagnose Post-Traumatic Stress Disorder and related conditions and then obtain specialized treatment.[132] In the I/DD system and in working with people with I/DD, things are quite different.

The factors in eligibility for services, the nature of services and supports themselves, powerful historical factors, and the dearth of specialized treatment open and ready to provide for a person with I/DD are just a few of the many things that have made this translation and adaptation difficult. Still relatively new in I/DD, though fully incorporated into Trauma Responsive Care, is the concept of universal precaution, borrowed from trauma-responsive systems of care for children. This concept is essential to minimizing the risk of re-traumatization when a crisis can place a child in services and perhaps even in substitute care while background information is yet being assembled. In I/DD, this concept allows an organization to move beyond trauma-informed and become trauma-responsive, regardless of how much of the story is known, treating everyone as if they could benefit from feeling safe, connected, and in control.

As a result, the advances in trauma-informed care have happened, by and large, where the services happen — with the provider. So, explicit policy around trauma in the I/DD sector is still rather basic, focusing primarily on increasing awareness through training grants and seeking creative application of trauma-informed concepts by including requirements to demonstrate those concepts in responses to grants and requests for proposals.

This does not mean the underlying concepts of trauma-informed and trauma-responsive approaches were totally new to the I/DD community. On the contrary, I/DD along with education has provided, over the past several decades, a rich and fertile soil for philosophies and approaches consumed with treating people better and helping them live their lives on their own terms. The major sweeps of policy in I/DD over recent decades have worked to move people with disabilities from institutional care into communities shared by all sorts of people through Medicaid waiver programs. Likewise, legislation like the Individuals with Disabilities Education

Act (IDEA) has helped to integrate schools and classrooms.[133] Beyond these larger policy milestones, our field has embraced a succession of philosophies and approaches that have moved us in the right direction: normalization, Person-Centered Planning, Gentle Teaching, positive psychology, and policies away from aversive behavioral techniques, just to name a few.

In truth, Trauma Responsive Care sits on a mountain of earlier and still vibrant innovations, now informed by an ever-widening scientific base in traumatology, attachment theory, polyvagal theory, and advances in the neurosciences generally.

So, when we seek to influence policy, we can rest assured we are already standing on firm ground. And, as your organization emerges from implementing Trauma Responsive Care, you are well-positioned to begin a deeper conversation with policymakers, especially as your outcomes begin to bear fruit.

Just like influencing internally and sustaining and strengthening our organizational commitment, leaders can cultivate habits of collaboration and communication outside of the organization.

### Talk With a New Voice Using Familiar Words

There are a few highly influential trends in I/DD that have captivated policy and become more and more a part of how we think about providing supports to people with disabilities. Two of them come to mind immediately, Person-Centered Planning and approaches and mechanisms to decrease and then eliminate aversive behavioral measures. Trauma Responsive Care harmonizes very well with these approaches. This means conversations about person-centered approaches, positive psychologies, like Gentle Teaching, and asset-based approaches to community building and change are already familiar to policymakers. Adding Trauma Responsive Care to these conversations and conveying the values of Trauma Responsive Care as values contained in these more established approaches will help others understand it better through association with concepts they already grasp.

This is really applying associative thinking habits discussed above to conversations with the larger community and with policymakers.

### Always Talk in Terms of Outcomes

Trauma Responsive Care is, ultimately, the core of any drive to do better. First, this means better outcomes, that is fewer of the less desirable things — like major unusual incidents, trips to emergency services, and harmful or destructive events — and a more positive, stable, and happy life for the people you're supporting. Second, this means a more satisfied, fulfilled, and stable workforce, and all that goes with it — reduced absenteeism, reduced turnover, increased staff satisfaction and investment. This is what you're shooting for. This high level of real quality is why you're implementing Trauma Responsive Care, and you're measuring outcomes to make sure you achieve it. Now, let the numbers speak for themselves.

Say, "When the people we support feel safe, connected, and in control, they're happier, healthier, and live better lives." Then show the numbers.

Say, "When employees feel safe, connected, and in control, they're happier, more productive, and better at their jobs." Then show the numbers.

Say, "When we implemented Trauma Responsive Care, we found it easier to align our mission with our customers' needs and the skills of our workforce. As a result, we have better business outcomes." Then show the numbers.

Policy has to positively impact every side of an issue: the recipient, the providers, and the general public. Policymakers have to consider the political climate and satisfy demand for a solid regulatory basis. If you talk about a "win–win–win" situation and you have the numbers, you will have influence.

### Build Collaborations

Some states have built public-private collaboratives to create conversations on how to improve services and supports. These collaborations can deepen conversations about and commitments to trauma-informed and trauma-responsive approaches. They can also morph into a collaborative infrastructure for training and information exchange.

If you know other providers who are implementing Trauma Responsive Care or have some other approach to addressing trauma, collaborate with them. Talk to them and learn from one another so you can support one another to create sustainable change.

These collaborative efforts are good for addressing problems stemming from the labor market and labor shortages, as well. We cannot compete very well on pay. Other service sector industries can respond to wage pressure much more quickly than providers of I/DD services can. Public-private policy dialogue, however, can help forge new ways to compete in the labor market. McKinsey & Company recently conducted a survey that investigated, among other things, why people are leaving jobs before they have other work lined up.[134] Among the top reasons were:

- Uncaring leadership
- Lack of meaningful work
- Lack of support for employee health and well-being

• Unreliable and unsupportive people at work
• Unsafe work environment
• Non-inclusive, unwelcoming, and disconnected community

All these areas are directly addressed by Trauma Responsive Care. We are in the business of meaningful work. But a response can only be scaled for impact throughout the industry through policy development. Advocate for this through collaborative action. Many voices are heard while a single voice is easily lost.

This gets us back to the beginning, asking and answering, from a wider policy perspective, why we should implement Trauma Responsive Care. Like many staff-driven helping industries, I/DD services is in a peculiar predicament. Both those served and those doing the serving live with a higher likelihood of exposure to trauma than the general population. Trauma-responsive organizations need to spread the word.

# acknowledgments

As part of my worldview, I believe all things are interconnected. So, the knowledge, experience, and wisdom (if I can claim any) leading up to and contained in this book are built on the knowledge, experience, and wisdom of so many who have taught me. From my distant past, I think of people like Mary Borchardt, my middle school English teacher; Robert S. Gorbold, D. Min., my childhood pastor; and Richard Besancon, Ph.D., my undergraduate philosophy professor. They all encouraged me in everything I did and cut me very little slack along the way. Unfortunately, they have all passed, or rest assured, I would make them read this book.

In more recent times, there are many people from whom I have learned so much. All of them have become part of my thinking on management and leadership, especially how these topics manifest themselves as we endeavor to include and support and love one another, which is the truest vocation of human services organizations.

I would like to specifically thank just a few of these "guiding lights," as I have felt them so forcefully in the time I have concentrated on writing this book.

First, I thank my children, Scott, Bryan, and Trisha, and Colin and Anna. They have all been very supportive — helping with research, for instance, on Crew Resource Management (Scott), or reading various versions to help me remove the parts I thought funny or useful but really weren't (Colin), or helping me think through the practical implications of some nascent idea (Bryan). *Thank you and I love you!*

I am also grateful to my parents, Barbara and Dalton Aldridge, and my sisters and brothers, Dawn Thomas, Suzanne and Dean Meece, and Geoffrey and Grant Aldridge-Duncan. *I feel your support every day, usually in a group text.*

I must also thank Marshall Towe, Jr. I've known him since we were teenagers, and he has granted me opportunities and experiences — and more importantly, friendship — I would not have otherwise had. *Thanks, Marshall!*

Thanks also to Jeanne Farr and everyone at the National Association for the Dually Diagnosed (NADD) for their enthusiastic support of this topic and my proposal for this book, not to mention their trust in me to pull it off. *Thanks, Jeanne, and thanks, NADD!*

Thanks also to Jennifer Scroggins, my editor, and Mark Sullivan, my designer. They have both been so kind and diligent, and their feedback has been invaluable. *Thanks, guys. You have no idea how wonderful you have made this whole process feel.*

Most importantly, however, I want to thank my partner at Aldridge Palay Consulting, Lara Palay. I am grateful beyond words for her work, her book, and her incredible mind — but most of all for her friendship. *Thank you, Lara.*

Finally, thank you, Debra, to whom this book is dedicated, in loving memory. *Debra R. Aldridge (October 4, 1957—November 10, 2015)*

# endnotes

1.  Aldridge, K. (1984). *God and Creativity: A Process Answer to Robert C. Neville's Critique of Process Theism.* [Unpublished master's thesis.] Northern Theological Seminary. It is amazingly unreadable!

2.  This line is from the song "Won't Get Fooled Again," written by Pete Townshend, although it most likely has a deeper history. The song was recorded by The Who and released on their album *Who's Next* in 1971.

3.  This quote has been altered to use gender-neutral language.

4.  This event is known as Merkle's Boner and is still hotly debated today. There are numerous sources for this story, including Baseball-Almanac. com and Baseball-Reference.com. It was also featured in *Baseball*, a documentary by Ken Burns. As for what happened next, news traveled fast but sporadically, and the police were called in to get the umpires out safely. The game could not be resumed and the Cubs won a makeup game on October 8. The Giants were edged out of the National League pennant by one game that year — by the Chicago Cubs. The Cubs went on to face Detroit in the World Series for the second year in a row and won in five games, for the second year in a row. After winning it twice, Chicago did not return to the World Series until 1945 and did not win it again until 2016, 108 years later. Fred Merkle had a full career, playing another nineteen years in the majors, part of that time, ironically, in a Cubs uniform.

5.  Palay, L. (2021). *The Way Through: Trauma Responsive Care for Intellectual and Developmental Disability Professionals.* NADD Press.

6.  Most notably for this field see Harvey, K. (2009). *Positive Identity Development: An Alternative Treatment Approach for Individuals with Mild and Moderate Intellectual Disabilities.* NADD Press; and McGilvery, S. (2018). *The Identification and Treatment of Trauma in Individuals with Developmental Disabilities.* NADD Press.

7.   Keesler, J. M. (2014). A Call for the Integration of Trauma-Informed Care Among Intellectual and Developmental Disability Organizations," *Journal of Policy and Practice in Intellectual and Developmental Disabilities, 11* (1), 34–42.

8.   Spencer, N., Devereux, E., Wallace, A., Sundrum, R., Shenoy, M., Bacchus, C., and Stuart Logan, S. (2005). Disabling Conditions and Registration for Child Abuse and Neglect: A Population-Based Study, *Pediatrics, 116,* 609–613.

9.   Sullivan, P. M., and Knutson, J. F. (2000). Maltreatment and disabilities: A population-based epidemiological study. *Child Abuse and Neglect.* 24, 1257–1273.

10.   Keesler.

11.   Fletcher, R., et al., (Eds.) (2007). *Diagnostic Manual-Intellectual Disability: A Clinical Guide for Diagnosis of Mental Disorders in Persons with Intellectual Disability.* NADD Press, 2.

12.   Fletcher, 2. The figure of 40.9% was rounded up by this author.

13.   These first four stats are from the National Core Indicators 2018–2019 Survey: https://www.nationalcoreindicators.org.

14.   The figure of 25.9% was rounded up by this author. In contrast, 11.4% of people without disabilities live in poverty. It should also be noted that this statistic is not specific to but inclusive of cognitive disabilities. These statistics were taken from https://www.statista.com/statistics/979003/disability-poverty-rate-us/.

15.   These three statistics on sexual assault were taken from Erika Harrell, "Crime Against Persons with Disabilities, 2009–2015 — Statistical tables," Bureau of Justice Statistics, July 2017, NCJ 250632. https:// www.bjs. gov/content/pub/pdf/capd0915st.pdf. According to the U.S. Department of Justice statistics, in 2011, 2.7 per 1,000 persons with a disability experienced rape or a sexual assault compared to 0.9 per 1,000 people without a disability; 36.7 per 1,000 experienced some kind of assault compared to 16.7 per 1,000 of people without a disability. Researchers estimate that only one out of thirty cases of sexual abuse gets reported.

16. That's me; I said that. It is my belief that in the broad spectrum of social welfare public policy, disability policy is, largely, not only its own pie, but rather it has a slice of every other policy pie and should be treated as such. The segregation of people with disabilities from everything from healthcare to employment is reinforced by the segregation of disability policy. Although there are indications of this changing, it is not changing quickly enough and represents a basic error in how we do policy for people with disabilities.

17. Sobsey, D. (1994). *Violence in the Lives of People with Disabilities: The End of Silent Acceptance?* P.H. Brooks. Sobsey is one of the pioneers of addressing how frequently people with I/DD experience trauma.

18. Palay, 24–25.

19. Palay, 60.

20. Fans of C.S. Lewis's *Chronicles of Narnia* will recall that the Pevensie children encountered the magic wardrobe while evacuated during the war.

21. National Council for Behavioral Health: https://www.thenationalcouncil.org/wp-content/uploads/2013/05/Trauma-infographic.pdf?daf=375ateTbd56.

22. Elliott, D. M. (1997). Traumatic Events: Prevalence and delayed recall in the general population." *Journal of Consulting and Clinical Psychology*, 65(5), 811–820. This particular study found an overall prevalence of 72%.

23. These figures are taken from the National Institutes of Health: https://www.nimh.nih.gov/health/statistics/post-traumatic-stress-disorder-ptsd. They cite Harvard Medical School's National Comorbidity Study: Harvard Medical School, 2007. National Comorbidity Survey (NCS), August 21, 2017. Retrieved from https:// www.hcp.med.harvard.edu/ncs/index.php. Data Tables 2 (12-month prevalence DSM-IV/WMH-CIDI disorders by sex and cohort) and 1 (Lifetime prevalence DSM-IV/WMH-CIDI disorders by sex and cohort).

24. These numbers are from Zippia, a career and jobs site: https://www.zippia.com/direct-support-professional-jobs/demographics/. The rounded demographics are roughly 13% Latino, 10% African

American, 7% Asian, and 3% other. Obviously, as we draw from a local workforce, these "macro" demographics probably do not accurately reflect any given "micro" environments.

25. Tolin, D. F., and Foa, E. (2006). Sex differences in trauma and posttraumatic stress disorder: a quantitative review of 25 years of research, *Psychol Bull*. 132(6), 959–992. https://doi. org/10.1037/0033-2909.132.6.959.

26. Kilpatrick, D. G., Resnick, H. S., Milanak, M. E., Miller, M. W., Keyes, K. M., and Friedman, M. J. (2013). National estimates of exposure to traumatic events and PTSD prevalence using DSM-IV and DSM-5 criteria. *Journal of Trauma Stress*, 26(5), 537–547. https://doi.org/10.1002/jts.21848.

27. Sendler, D. J., Ruthowska, A., and Makara-Studzinska, M. (2016). How the exposure to trauma has hindered physicians' capacity to heal: prevalence of PTSD among healthcare workers. *The European Journal of Psychiatry*, 30(4).

28. Serrano-Ripoll, M. J., Meneses-Echavez, J. F., Ricci-Cabello, I., Fraile-Navarro, D., Fiol-deRoque, M. A., Pastor-Moreno, G., Castro, A., Ruiz-Pérez, I., Campos, R. Z., Gonçalves-Bradley, D. C. (2020). Impact of viral epidemic outbreaks on mental health of healthcare workers: a rapid systematic review and meta-analysis. *Journal of Affect Disorders*, 277, 347–357.

As mentioned, these analyses are prior to the pandemic. Through the pandemic and in its aftermath, these numbers, including the prevalence of things like vicarious trauma, and empathetic and moral injury, probably have expanded. The true impact of the global pandemic, including persistently higher prevalence of these negative effects, will not be known for some time.

29. Please note, if you don't know from experience, that it can be quite stressful for anyone to work closely with a population as traumatized as people struggling with disabilities. This stress can manifest as things like vicarious or secondary trauma, compassion fatigue, empathetic distress or injury, and burnout and can go unnoticed, unsupported, and untreated.

This is why a systematic approach to supporting our workforce, beyond the scope of this book, is so necessary. Leadership in provider organizations should view efforts to provide support to this workforce and to support their own emotional self-care as part of risk mitigation. If your agency does not have a thorough and written risk-mitigation plan that includes the emotional support of your staff, develop one now.

30. Brisson, D., McCune, S., Wilson, J. H., Speer, S. R., McCrae, J. S., and Calhoun, K. H. (2019). A Systematic Review of the Association between Poverty and Biomarkers of Toxic Stress. *Journal of Evidence-Based Social Work, 17*(6), 696–713.

31. Keesler.

32. These stats are taken from research conducted by the Institute of Community Integration at the University of Minnesota along with the National Association of Direct Support Professionals. View the full report at https://ici.umn.edu/covid19-survey.

33. Ritter, T. (2014). *Alignment² [Alignment Squared]: Driving Competitiveness and Growth Through Business Model Excellence.* The CBS Competitiveness Platform. Copenhagen Business School. Figure 1.1 is adapted from Ritter's Business Model Square, 15.

34. Heraclitus of Ephesus was a pre-Socratic philosopher (540–480, BCE). We know little about him, and his writings survive only in snippets others have used in their writings, mostly to argue against him. We do know that personally he could be kind of a jerk and that his most significant contribution to the foundations of Greek philosophy is the idea of change as a basic characteristic of the universe. He also said something like this: "You can never step in the same river twice, for you have changed, and so has the river."

35. Some forms of this story have been reported in the guise of actual transcripts of Stephen Covey's (1989) famous book *Seven Habits of Highly Effective People.* Free Press. The story goes back in some form as early as the 1930s! Here is a site with more detail if you're interested. https://www.snopes.com/ fact-check/the-obstinate-lighthouse/.

36. From a wider perspective and from the Navy's point of view, it's a story of a persistent, nagging past that never seems to completely disappear. Every time it appears in print or pops up in an interview, even as an illustration, there's a good chance someone somewhere will call the Navy for more information or for corroboration.

37. Netting, F. E., Kettner, P. M., McMurtry, S. L., and Thomas, M. L. (2012). *Social Work Macro Practice* (5th ed). Pearson, 7.

38. As I am writing, *The Economist* stated that Cadillac reportedly told its dealers they will need to spend an estimated $200,000 in retooling and retraining as the General Motors brand moves to electric. (2021, October 20). Servicing and repairing electric cars requires new skills. *The Economist*. https://www.economist.com/science-and-technology/servicing-and-repairing-electric-cars-requires-new-skills/21805752. And the Ohio Department of Developmental Disabilities is experimenting with the use of robots in three service sites with people with I/DD. Yeah, big changes.

39. Harris, M., and Fallot, R. D. (Eds.) (2001). *Using Trauma Theory to Design Service Systems*. Jossey-Bass.

40. There is, as you might guess, an underlying debate in the change management literature, as well as in psychology generally, as to whether attitude changes behavior or behavior changes attitude. We don't need to answer this question definitively because we already know the two are inseparably interconnected. Impacting attitude so it can, in turn, impact behavior, and vice versa, is hardwired into our assumptions about creating viable and sustainable change.

41. In 2020, I gave a presentation on responding to the pandemic in which I said the organizational weaknesses we take into a major crisis tend to get amplified by the crisis ("Post-Pandemic Planning: Understanding the New Normal," the 37th Annual NADD National conference). Given the fact that high turnover was virtually a universal "weakness" in this field going into the pandemic, my insight would not have been welcome news under any circumstances. Reality, as it turns out, is even more dire, as the pandemic has wreaked unprecedented havoc on the labor market as a

whole, impacting work habits and perspectives throughout. This fact has not been lost on me and I have taken it to heart as I write this book. Katz, L. F., and Krueger, A. B. (1992). The Effect of the Minimum Wage on the Fast-Food Industry. *Industrial and Labor Relations Review*, 46, 6–21.

42. Peters, T., and Waterman, R. H. (1982). *In Search of Excellence: Lessons from America's Best-Run Companies.* Warner. This book is still an absolute must-read. The authors' abstraction of insights across industries has also made it virtually as applicable today as it was when it first came out. This book also introduced the McKinsey 7-S Framework, an extremely effective framework for assessing an organization. A cautionary tale into the relentless nature of change: If you replicated this process today, you would not come up with the same list of companies.

43. Garvin, D. A., and Roberto, M. A. (2005). Change Through Persuasion. *Harvard Business Review*, February.

44. Does this method sound familiar? Daniel Coyle relays the story of the Allen Curve wonderfully. See Coyle, D. (2018). *The Culture Code: The Secrets of Highly Successful Groups.* Bantam, 69–70. See also Allen, T. J. (1977). *Managing the Flow of Technology.* MIT Press.

45. Kotter, J. P. (1995). Leading Change: Why Transformation Efforts Fail.

46. *Harvard Business Review*, March.

47. Garvin and Roberto talk about convincing people the organization is on death's door as part of this important differentiation of past from proposed future.

48. Beer, M. Eisenstat, R., and Spector, B. (1990). Why Change Programs Don't Produce Change. *Harvard Business Review*, November. Beer, et al. talk about this sense of urgency as mobilizing commitment through joint diagnosis of the problem.

49. The SAT is the Scholastic Aptitude Test, used in college admissions, though it is waning as of late. It is chock full of these relational multiple-choice questions: "A" is to "B" as "1" is to "____."

50. See Garvin and Roberto and Beer, et al.

51. See Gillett, E., and Stenfert-Kroese, B. (2003). Investigating Organizational Culture: A comparison of a "high"- and a "low"-performing residential unit for people with intellectual disabilities. *Journal of Applied Research in Intellectual Disabilities*, 16, 279–284. The authors conclude a possible link between culture and quality. Also see Bloom, S. (2006). Organizational Stress as a Barrier to Trauma-Sensitive Change and System Transformation. National Association of State Mental Health Program Directors. https://connectingparadigms.org/wp-content/uploads/2019/05/21360-Organizational_Stress_as_a_Barrier_to_Trauma-Informed-Bloom.pdf.

52. Except for the 1906 Chicago Cubs. That year they won 116 of 152 games — the most winning record (by percentage) in baseball history — even better than the '27 Yankees, with "Murderers' Row" in its full powers. The Yankees won only 110 of 155 games that year. So there. And, no, I'm not going to mention Seattle's 2001 season with 116 wins because I don't want to.

53. Palay. The lesson of maximizing early wins is dominated by stories at first and then later, by stories and data. Therefore, in this section my examples are much less generic, as in other lessons of this chapter, and much more specific to Trauma Responsive Care.

54. From *The Art of Poetry*.

55. See https://lessonslearned.faa.gov/ll_main.cfm?TabID=3&LLID=8.

56. See https://lessonslearned.faa.gov/ll_main.cfm?TabID=1&LLID=52.

57. See https://lessonslearned.faa.gov/ll_main.cfm?TabID=1&LLID=42.

58. I like the term *customer*. When I was an exec, I used to talk to incoming employees during their training and I would always say "customers" instead of "consumers" for a very simple reason. I would tell them that consumers are an abstract group without a face. We work with people — customers — and customers can fire us.

59. Ritter, T.

60. This "If — And — Then" statement structure is a variation of a logical syllogism, originally developed by Aristotle. That philosophy degree is paying off!

61. Palay, Chapter Six covers the CALMER Skills (83–96). They are: Check In, Accept, Loving-Kindness, Mindful, Express, and Respond.

62. Backward mapping from outcomes is part of a larger approach to managing change called Theory of Change. "Theory of Change is essentially a comprehensive description and illustration of how and why a desired change is expected to happen in a particular context." It is a good tool for mission-driven organizations because it provides a way to connect sometimes rather vague outcomes, like, in this case, a more stable life, with concrete actions that support the goal and increase the likelihood of it happening — what its proponents call "the middle road." See the Center for Theory of Change: https://www.theoryofchange.org.

63. The life and work of John McGee were instrumental in the formation of Trauma Responsive Care. I knew John for a number of years and was blessed to work closely with him in Ohio in the final few years of his life when I was with the Ohio Department of Developmental Disabilities. His seminal book, *Gentle Teaching: A Nonaversive Approach for Helping Persons with Mental Retardation* (1987) is still a great read, in spite of its now out-of-date terminology. Human Services Press, University of Michigan.

64. Harvey, K.

65. Palay, 61.

66. Palay, 24–25.

67. Palay, 60.

68. Palay, 61.

69. As Palay has said, "If you're working with someone, say, 50 years old or older, given the state of our recordkeeping, the tumultuous history of our services to people, and given what questions a clinician would look for today — they could have been raised by wolves for all we can tell."

70. This chapter is best read in light of the companion to this book (Palay).

71. Servant leadership is a concept in leadership and power covered from numerous perspectives in numerous books by numerous authors. It started with Robert K. Greenleaf's (1977) collection of essays published under the title *Servant Leadership: A Journey into the Nature of Legitimate Power and Greatness*. Paulist.

72. Kotter, J. P. (1995). Leading Change: Why Transformation Efforts Fail. *Harvard Business Review*, March.

73. I'm sorry, I can't resist a bit of management theory. An important thing to remember about the management role is that managers are quite often held responsible for things they cannot control. This is part of planning and forecasting. As the manager of a shoe store, one may think boots will be big again, so they order a lot. If it turns out the world, or at least this manager's part of it, has grown tired of boots and suddenly this store's inventory does not match the market, what happens? As they work to correct the emerging sales slump they had no control over, it's obvious they could not be blamed for the public's fickle relationship with boots. However, they still have to answer for the slump in sales, and their bonus, or lack thereof, will reflect that responsibility.

74. Incidentally, this concept of alignment could be one of the most important factors for survival in a post-pandemic world. See Ritter, T., and Pedersen, C. L. (2020). Assessing Coronavirus's Impact on your Business Model. *Harvard Business Review* digital article. https://hbr.org/2020/04/assessing-coronaviruss-impact-on-your-business-model.

75. Palay, pp. 83–96.

76. I have used these traditional business acronyms because, while not universal, they are ubiquitous. Some may use terms like *president* and a series of vice presidents of operations, people, finance, etc. It provides us with a common understanding of who exactly we're talking about.

77. Business guru Tom Peters gets at this idea rather directly: "The graveyard shift knows more about the company's problems with quality and service and about new competitors than the bosses do, all nine levels of them." Peters, T. (1987). *Thriving on Chaos: Handbook for a Management Revolution*. Harper Collins, 514.

78. Palay, 31–50.

79. From *The Builders.*

80. This measure of critical mass at 60% is not scientific but based on our experience working with organizations. We have also discerned, as discussed, that who benefits from this initial training drive is equally important — frontline supervisors are the linchpin. This rule-of-thumb number of 60% can be broken down in particular divisions or geographic areas. It's just a guideline, though, and as Trauma Responsive Care takes hold in various parts of your organization, you'll learn more about where to place additional resources.

81. I am tempted to use the metaphor of DNA, something like: "The object of the tasks of organizational investment is to infuse your organization's DNA with Trauma Responsive Care." Just as DNA functions in an organism, Trauma Responsive Care needs to become that basic set of information, instruction, and perspective that informs every decision throughout the organization. However, this metaphor is so overused and has lost so much of its power, I just can't bring myself to use it. But then, I guess I just did.

82. For nonprofit organizations, this list would also include board agendas and meeting minutes.

83. These lessons from Chapter Two, connected with the task of organizational investment, are "Institutionalize the Change" and "Evaluate Continually."

84. These lessons from Chapter Two, connected with the task of building sustainability, are "Communicate," "Build a Sense of Urgency," "Create a Vision," "Rely on Persuasion," "Nurture Change Where It Grows," and "Grab Short-Term Wins and Leverage Them."

85. Recall the phases of leadership communication discussed in Chapter Two: "Setting the stage, framing the change plan, managing the mood, and preventing backsliding." Garvin and Roberto (2005).

86. Not to mention the Four R's.

87. This might not be comfortable, but it might be a good time to remind managers that, for the most part, they are a drain on the organization

— bosses generally don't produce many billable units, if any. So, management should always be concerned with adding value with every decision.

88. These distinctions are not in any way pure. You can think of it on a continuum with activities containing varying degrees of *causing to be done* at one end and *actually doing* at another.

89. For the purposes of our discussion, in a human services organization, a service-based division and a region-based division look the same. They can also have a distinct cultural identity from another division doing the same service. In fact, I have worked with organizations that divided first by service and then by region, so each division covered the same geographic area as well as the other way around, by region and then by service. In that case, different services made up subdivisions.

90. There is a very interesting discussion of this topic from the perspective of systems in Jamshid Gharajedaghi's (2006) book *Systems Thinking: Managing Chaos and Complexity: A Platform for Designing Business Architecture.* Butterworth-Heinemann, 6–8. Gharajedaghi cites Womack, J. P., Jones, D. T., and Roos, D. (1990). *The Machine That Changed the World.* Free Press.

91. I know what you're thinking: What kind of father would sell an AMC Gremlin to his own child? But it's not like that; my father loves me. He picked it up for us for $500 and took less from us to buy it. And I used those tools — a lot.

92. Teams are not perfect. In fact, they can have a tendency to sap their own collaborative powers through problems with competition, lopsided motivation, and productivity lags. I often heard this complaint from graduate students doing group assignments, frustrated that it was easier for a few to do all the work even to the benefit of more lazy members. Although I was more pedagogical in my response, I basically told them, "Welcome to the real world." See Diane Coutu's discussion with researcher Hackman, J. R. on his book, *Leading Teams,* printed in the *Harvard Business Review.* Coutu, D. (2009). Why Teams Don't Work: An Interview with J. Richard Hackman. *Harvard Business Review.* May.

93. *Webster's New Explorer Dictionary* (1999). Merriam-Webster, 545.

94. Dictionary.com. Tool. https://www.dictionary.com.

95. Dictionary.com. Tool.

96. Here's a mnemonic familiar to anyone who played a musical instrument: Every Good Boy Deserves Fudge — EGBDF are the line notes of the treble clef. The space notes? FACE!

97. Palay.

98. Dennett, D. C. (1991). *Consciousness Explained*. Little, Brown, 200–202.

99. Dawkins, R. (1976). *The Selfish Gene*. Oxford University Press, 206. Also quoted by Dennett.

100. More often than not these days, you will hear the term in connection with sales strategy, usually business to business (B2B) or non-retail sales. The idea is the same, however. The salesperson identifies someone inside the firm he or she is selling to, hopefully in a decision-making capacity, who loves the service or product the salesperson is selling. This *internal champion* then becomes the informal "seller" or advocate of the service or product inside the targeted firm.

101. This webinar was part of a series sponsored by the American Network of Community Options and Resources (ANCOR) and the National Association of Dual Diagnosis (NADD). I am proud to say that the latter, NADD, is my publisher.

102. Whitehead, A. N. (1929, 1978). *Process and Reality: An Essay in Cosmology*. Free Press, 339. This work is the published version of the Gifford Lectures, hosted jointly by the universities of Edinburgh, Glasgow, and St. Andrews, delivered in 1927. In my estimation, it is one of the most important philosophical works in Western thought.

103. From *On Modern Poetry*.

104. The quote is, "Perfection is the enemy of the good," and it is generally attributed to Voltaire. Ratcliffe, S. (2011). *Concise Oxford Dictionary of Quotations*. Oxford University Press, 389. Economist George Stigler said, "If you've never missed a plane, you're spending too much time at the airport." You get the point.

105. A SWOT analysis is a straightforward framework for assessing one's competitive position in the world. The acronym stands for Strengths, Weaknesses, Opportunities, Threats.

106. Aldridge Palay has developed an organizational tool for human services organizations that works very well with I/DD services providers. Find it at www.aldridgepalay.com. However, you can build your own framework or checklist by starting with the basic tenants of Trauma Responsive Care contained in this book and in Palay's *The Way Through*.

107. I am borrowing the phrase "veil of ignorance" from philosopher John Rawls. To be fair, I'm borrowing the direct meaning, as in "act as if you don't know." Rawls used the phrase with this direct meaning in his "original position" thought experiment on social contract theory. I can hear you say, dear reader, "That's not really the point of this book, though, is it?" So, I will simply give the citation and be done. Rawls, J. (1999). *A Theory of Justice*. (Rev. ed.). Harvard University Press.

108. A team approach here, even though the project manager will also be heavily involved, will help a great deal if you use a more general framework as opposed to an existing checklist. There is always a balance of the objective, quantifiable kind of information and the more subjective, qualifiable kind of information. With a larger subjective element, having more people to discuss the issues and reach some consensus is easier and will arrive at a sounder conclusion.

109. Palay.

110. In these discussions, I am consistently referring to these teams as distinct and separate teams. Remember our discussion on teams in Chapter Six. These "teams" are more accurately a gathering of similar tasks and may therefore, depending on your circumstances, especially the size of your organization, be the same group of people or have overlapping membership and so look more like a Venn diagram than standalone circles.

111. Palay's book contains a wonderful discussion of adrenalized and sympathetic states to moderate threats and also more severe neuro-physical reactions like fight, flight, freeze, and fawn, along with collapse and dissociation. See Palay, Chapter Two: Trauma 101, 11–29.

112. Values in Action Institute on Character has a very helpful (and free) survey to identify a person's character strengths. See https://www.via character.org.

113. In trainings and consultations, Lara Palay often points out that when you're running from a bear, the higher cognitive functions used in identifying the physical and behavioral characteristics of a brown versus a black bear are not necessary to safety and survival and so are offline, so to speak.

114. Chesterton, G. K. (1910, 2021). *What's Wrong with the World*. Sofia Institute Press, 186. Chesterton identified this statement as "the prime truth of woman, the universal mother."

115. Another "borrowed" philosophical phrase. This one from British philosopher Gilbert Ryle.

116. Will your mission and value statement necessarily change? No, they may not change. However, you should consider two things here. First, this is a great opportunity to launch new mission and value statements to really anchor the change. Second, even if the words don't change, the interpretation must change and so must be retrained and reinforced. This is sort of a litmus test: If you don't think you need to reinterpret your mission and values statements, you are probably not thinking of deep enough change. If you are a team leader or division head and you're trying to make your own unit or division more responsive, then you should probably think about developing your own internal mission and value statements.

117. How powerful is this organization momentum? Once upon a time, there was a company called Enron. Enron, in the face of bad and fraudulent management, wound down operations so fast that employees who were laid off continued to get paid for several months after they were laid off. In some cases, employees without direct deposit simply walked to their old desks in a mostly empty building, saying hello to the security guard, and retrieved their continuing paychecks. The checks were delivered to their old desks through the inter-office mail system, still operating even after whole sectors of the company were shuttered. It seems that most of the people responsible for processing layoffs were themselves laid off,

so the system, following built-in policies and procedures, continued to function quite well. Evidently other systems, like drawing on cash reserves and existing lines of credit, also continued to function. It took years to untangle.

118. There is an interesting project, based at the University of London, that houses the archives of the Ministry of Information and research into its work. This shady government organization was the basis for George Orwell's Ministry of Truth in his great novel *1984*.

119. This chart is included to demonstrate the graphic presentation of outcomes. However, it reflects actual results experienced by an agency that implemented Trauma Responsive Care in 2016–2017. This graph was taken from the final report of that project.

120. This is taken from the book of Isaiah, a prophet in Jewish and Christian Scripture. Though not in the Qur'an, Isaiah, or Ishaʻyā, is revered in other Islamic texts. This translation is from the *New Revised Standard Version* (Deutero) Isaiah: 43:19a.

121. This experiment was part of a study that developed and tested three "small scale interventions." It was conducted by the Happier, Healthier Professionals Research project of What Works for Children's Social Care in Great Britain. The full report can be found at https://whatworks-csc.org.uk/wp-content/uploads/WWCSC_Happier-Healthier-Professionals-evaluation_March2021_v2.pdf.

122. A small article in the Bartleby column of *The Economist* summarizes a few other studies out of Harvard, King's College, London, and others. In one study, workers were randomly and secretly instructed to do some kindness to a coworker. The attitudes, perceptions, and performance of both the receivers and givers improved. Bartleby (2022). The power of small gestures. *The Economist,* May 28, 58.

123. This is slightly tongue in cheek. Obviously, bosses cannot be best friends with everyone, and there are some people you just don't click with. However, a good manager does need the capacity to rise above these personal feelings and be able to connect with all their staff in some way and find some level of genuine appreciation of their contribution.

124. Trauma Responsive Care can thrive under just about any overarching management model. There are some management models, however, that provide more barriers to being truly responsive than others. In particular, I am referring to practices that lean toward a more authoritarian model of management — strong chains of command with a stress on the giving and following of directives. It's not that these traits are bad or wrong in themselves. It's that the more authoritarian a management culture is, the more it tends to focus on a particular personality type to thrive — it is ultimately self-limiting. This does not translate into a lack of structure or concrete procedure. This can be advantageous and even necessary, like in healthcare, for example. In terms of management style, the lack of authoritarian management does not translate into a lack of control of the management process. Also, any open or more responsive management structure or style does not condone a loose approach to quality, safety, or the regulatory foundation of the industry.

125. Palay, Chapter Six: The CALMER Skills, 83–96.

126. Adler, M. J. (1985). *Ten Philosophical Mistakes: Basic Errors in Modern Thought.* Simon and Schuster.

127. Palay, 88–91.

128. Covey.

129. I have always heard this as a Yogi Berra quote, but I am told, by the website Quoteinvestigator.com, that its origins lie in the late 1930s with Danish politician Karl Kristian Steincke. At any rate, we will acknowledge that Yogi borrowed the wisdom. Incidentally, Yogi also observed that "the future is not what it used to be."

130. Associative thinking as a phenomenon: https://dictionary.apa.org/associative-thinking.

131. SAMHSA is a division of the U.S. Department of Health and Human Services. https://www.samhsa.gov.

132. The field of specialized treatment is still relatively young and evolving rapidly. For a great synopsis of the field and a good barometer of the direction of the field, see Van der Kolk, B. (2015). *The Body Keeps the Score: Brain, Mind, and Body in the Healing of Trauma.* Penguin.

133. The legislation was originally enacted as the Education for All Handicapped Children's Act in 1975. It was reauthorized and expanded in 1990 and renamed the Individuals with Disabilities Education Act then. See https://sites.ed.gov/idea/.

134. The Great Attrition/Great Attraction survey, by McKinsey & Company, asked employees who left a job during 2021 without other work lined up why they left. This survey was in the middle of what economists have called the Great Resignation, a marked increase in job departures as opposed to job shifts (from one employer to another). Although this new quest for meaning at work was definitely spurred by the pandemic and will subside over time, it appears to have become a sustained characteristic of labor market behavior. Various graphs from the study have been publicized in social media through May and June of 2022. For information on the survey and other findings, go to the McKinsey & Company website: https://www.mckinsey.com/business-functions/people-and-organizational-performance/our-insights/great-attrition-or-great-attraction-the-choice-is-yours.

## About the Author

Kevin Aldridge, MA, has more than 30 years of experience in human services, mostly in the I/DD and mental health sectors. He has vast experience in management, including running operations in Ohio for a national service provider in I/DD and mental health services. Kevin also served as Assistant Deputy Director for policy for the Ohio Department of Developmental Disabilities for four years. He taught courses in organizational and community change, social justice policy, strategic planning, and research, among other topics, at the Ohio State University College of Social Work. He has consulted on change management and team organization for global Fortune 100 companies. Kevin is a founding partner of Aldridge Palay Consulting. He serves on the boards of the Coalition on Homelessness and Housing in Ohio (COHHIO) and Creative Housing Inc. and speaks widely on topics such as organizational change, management, policy, and other issues. Kevin lives in Grandview Heights, Ohio, with his two cats. He enjoys reading, travel, kayaking, and backpacking — oh yeah, and baseball.

CPSIA information can be obtained
at www.ICGtesting.com
Printed in the USA
BVHW051515100123
655977BV00027B/271